Confederate
Statues and
Memorialization

HISTORY
IN THE HEADLINES

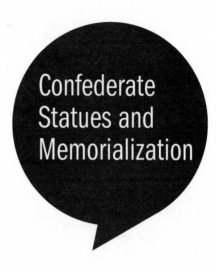

Confederate
Statues and
Memorialization

EDITED BY Catherine Clinton

The University of Georgia Press   *Athens*

This publication is made possible in part through a grant from
the Bradley Hale Fund for Southern Studies

Permissions credits for previously published material
appear on pages 175–76 and constitute an extension
of this copyright page.

Library of Congress Cataloging-in-Publication Data
Names: Clinton, Catherine, 1952– editor.
Title: Confederate statues and memorialization / edited by
    Catherine Clinton.
Other titles: History in the Headlines (Athens, Ga.)
Description: Athens : The University of Georgia Press, [2019] |
    Series: History in the Headlines
Identifiers: LCCN 2018054034| ISBN 9780820355559
    (hardcover : alk. paper) | ISBN 9780820355573 (pbk. : alk.
    paper) | ISBN 9780820355566 (ebook)
Subjects: LCSH: Soldiers' momuments—Southern States.
Classification: LCC E645 .C697 2019 | DDC 973.7/6—dc23
LC record available at https://lccn.loc.gov/2018054034

To the memory of
Heather Heyer
(1985–2017)

Contents

Acknowledgments

I would like to begin by thanking the hundreds of scholars who have contributed to this important discussion—at conferences, in classrooms, and most vibrantly, in the headlines. The series editors and volume editor owe a great deal to so many of these historians engaged in ongoing debates, particularly those who assisted us with getting their articles reprinted. We are particularly grateful to W. Fitzhugh Brundage, Karen Cox, Gary W. Gallagher, and Nell Irvin Painter, who took part in the initial round table for our series, allowing our glimmer of an idea to grow into full-fledged being— and helping us realize our hopes for this volume.

Without the gentle prodding and invaluable input of Mick Gusinde-Duffy (lo, those many coffees and lunches over the years!) and the ongoing and generous support of Lisa Bayer, this project would have remained on the back burner. We salute the designers, publicists, copyeditors—indeed, the entire team—at the University of Georgia Press, who have tirelessly labored to bring this book to print.

The editor wishes to acknowledge two invaluable research assistants: Deliliah Hernandez and Dr. Katherine K. Walters. Delilah attended the round table and provided excellent assistance on transcription and additional research. Dr. Walters was incredibly patient and tenacious in tracking down permissions and bibliographic information and in locating illustrative material for our web component. Both have been heroic in the face of a demanding, and too often dilatory, employer: many thanks.

Finally, Steve Berry provided inspiration and assistance at critical moments, and the series leans on him heavily for expertise and innovation.

My students at the University of Texas in San Antonio have provided me with a wonderful classroom laboratory to try out Civil War debates, while my department remains generous with assistance, including with travel funds to complete my work. Friends in San Antonio have been wonderfully supportive, and I want to single out three in particular—Nick Coates, George Byers, and Jason Johnson—who have endured my deliberations on matters great and small during the bumpy road to complete this project. And finally, to my two sons, Drew and Ned Colbert, who have contributed so much to my career over the years, including photographing monuments and forwarding articles—all the while providing cheer and companionship for the mother who has dragged them to Civil War reenactments from the age of four! Jim Downs, my son by another mother (the incredible Connie), provides ongoing energy and inspiration—and has been a remarkable comrade, co-conspirator, and collaborator for decades. I remain in his debt and grateful for his generosity. Hats off to all who continue on the journey and make me want to keep on keeping on.

Catherine Clinton
San Antonio, Texas
September 2018

Confederate
Statues and
Memorialization

Introduction

The American Civil War has dominated the historical landscape—and for the past century, it has often decorated the literal landscape of the United States. With the military surrender at Appomattox in April 1865, the battle over the retelling of the war and the re-framing of the conflict began. Alternate and clashing visions of this era have been a staple within American historical curriculum and contribute to the continuing boom in Civil War studies. Revisionism and memorialization has become a prolonged and often contentious process that once involved thousands of dedicated veterans—those who had been on the front lines, as well as those on the home front.

Indeed, veterans of the home front were most closely involved in issues of memorialization, particularly within the defeated Confederate states. Legions of men and women were dedicated to valorizing those sacrificed, cheering returning heroes, and fashioning public spaces into elaborate and permanent reminders of heroic deeds. This was the launching of the Lost Cause, a multi-generational initiative that shone the spotlight on the Confederate bid for nationhood and the glorified white southerners who had declared independence and fought to maintain racial slavery.[1]

---

1   See Rollin G. Osterweis, *The Myth of the Lost Cause, 1865–1900* (New York: Archon Books, 1973); Charles Reagan Wilson, *Baptized in Blood: The Religion of the Lost Cause, 1865–1920* (Athens: University of Georgia Press, 1982); Gaines M. Foster, *Ghosts of the Confederacy: Defeat, the Lost Cause, and the Emergence of the New South, 1865–1913* (New York: Oxford University Press, 1987); and Karen L. Cox,

White southerners were distressed by Reconstruction. In addition to the rise of paramilitary organizations such as the Ku Klux Klan, white southerners banded together to form associations such as the United Confederate Veterans, the United Daughters of the Confederacy, and Ladies Memorial Associations. These groups were vigilant, trying to rephrase the conflict into a "War for Southern Independence" or more infamously the "War of Northern Aggression." Granite and marble embellishments became a noble cause for many veterans and their descendants, as this monument movement effectively redecorated public squares, courthouse entrances, and parks across the nation, but most particularly the former Confederate states in the South.

During the past fifty years, since the Civil War centenary, debates over these memorialization efforts have escalated. The impact of these marble men, with white gleaming arms and armaments, remains a source of bitter division. Conflicting opinions have given much offense and in some cases led to violence—and even loss of life.

Mary Boykin Chesnut, Augusta Evans, and many other scribbling southern white sisters who endured Confederate surrender only wanted the fighting to stop. But with Yankee rule, and a general malaise, many women were drafted or volunteered to take up the pen, as men had taken up the sword. Chesnut and her cohorts decided they would write themselves out of defeat. In a sense they fought to "win the peace" after losing the war. By embellishing the plantation epic, by vigorous pursuit of sentimental yet partisan memoirs, they resurrected and reinvigorated their claim on the

---

Dixie's Daughters: The United Daughters of the Confederacy and the Preservation of Confederate Culture (Gainesville: University Press of Florida, 2003).

Civil War's legacy. They proposed the battle over slavery had been only a sidebar for the "brother's war" to preserve antebellum values against Yankee encroachments and depredations.

This band of sisters set out to create a literary canon that would preserve and perpetuate this *Confederado* point of view. For the next half-century, and into the twentieth, southern fiction and memoir highlighted white women's distinctive roles, discussed in detail in Edmund Wilson's *Patriotic Gore: Studies of the Literature of the American Civil War* (1960), Anne Goodwyn Jones's *Tomorrow Is Another Day: The Woman Writer in the South, 1859–1936* (1981), Sarah Gardner's *Blood and Irony: Southern White Women's Narratives of the Civil War, 1861–1937* (2003), and Caroline Janney's *Remembering the Civil War: Reunion and the Limits of Reconciliation* (2013).[2]

With Confederate defeat, Augusta Evans proclaimed in October 1865, "I shudder at the bitter, bitter feelings I find smoldering in my heart. . . . I feel that I have no country, no home, no hope in coming years, and I brood over our hallowed precious past."[3] She wrote indignantly to a friend in October 1866, a friend who suggested the war might have been a mistake: "The right of Secession is more holy than five years ago,—for now it has been sanctified—baptized

2 Edmund Wilson, *Patriotic Gore: Studies in the Literature of the American Civil War* (New York: Oxford University Press, 1962); Anne Goodwyn Jones, *Tomorrow Is Another Day: The Woman Writer in the South, 1859–1936* (Baton Rouge: Louisiana State University Press, 1981); Sarah Gardner, *Blood and Irony: Southern White Women's Narratives of the Civil War, 1861–1937* (Chapel Hill: University of North Carolina Press, 2003); and Caroline Janney, *Remembering the Civil War: Reunion and the Limits of Reconciliation* (Chapel Hill: University of North Carolina Press, 2013).
3 Elizabeth Moss, *Domestic Novelists of the Old South* (Baton Rouge: Louisiana State University Press, 1992), 8.

anew, with the blood of our Legion of Liberty's Martyrs."[4] Her devotion to this cause was religious, unwavering. As Gaines Foster and Charles Reagan Wilson have demonstrated, this evangelical fervor would only grow in the months and years that followed the war's bitter close. Meanwhile, a rising generation of white southern men would see the war as a crisis they would remedy through regional nationalism and white supremacy.[5]

The rise of social media, combined with a changing political climate, has accelerated the involvement of historians in the contemporary debates over memorialization. Yet not everyone has welcomed historians' engagement with these topics. Some have criticized historians both for making generalizations and for making false analogies to the past, arguing that historians ought to focus their attention on nuanced arguments in books and not try to cram their analysis into abbreviated commentary, such as op-eds, blogs, and podcasts. Others disagree; in fact, the *Washington Post* hired a cadre of young historians to lead a new online commentary section, Made By History, that draws on deep historical analyses to situate contemporary news (articles from which are included in both the bibliography and on our "Top Ten" list). Additionally, many historians have placed traditional publishing agendas on hold to create their own podcasts, blogs, and web pages. A new generation may curate their faculty profiles to make them more media savvy.

Professional organizations have also established special sessions at their annual meetings to discuss the increased role of historians as public intellectuals. History in the Headlines began as a feature at the Southern Historical Association (SHA) in November 2016

4 *A Southern Woman of Letters: The Correspondence of Augusta Jane Evans Wilson*, ed. Rebecca Grant Sexton (Columbia: University of South Carolina Press, 2002), 131.
5 Foster, *Ghosts of the Confederacy* ; C. R. Wilson, *Baptized in Blood* .

and continues to highlight scholars engaged with contemporary issues.[6] The Southern Historical Association at its origins was indeed one of the organizations that contributed to the perpetuation of the Confederate project. The organization's early leadership overinvested in the perpetuation of a "southern way of life," a perspective that included glorification of the Confederate cause and a predilection for white supremacy. In recent years, the SHA has done much to counter this early focus, mounting campaigns to place civil rights and fights for social justice at the forefront of organizational strategies for historical revisionism.

The role of historical studies has expanded exponentially over the past few decades. The ways and means of creating a platform for greater awareness of ongoing trends allows for dramatic developments. Younger scholars, working on their PhDs, might create more-informed decisions about current affairs. This is one of the most fertile eras for those who want to connect the past to the present, with multiple media platforms available to glean the widest possible audience.

Certainly the intertwining of topical issues and historical controversies has had an engrossing effect. Electronic history lists have developed traction, with H-NET (Humanities and Social Sciences Online) emerging roughly twenty-five years ago. Among the networks developed in H-NET, none has been more robust and exciting than H-CivWar. During its early days and for its first decade, the moderators of this online network would regularly suggest that another thread on Black Confederates be retired. Turf wars, not just online but in university classrooms and town squares, have

---

6   For the record, this initiative was created and piloted by the SHA president for 2016 and her program cochair, Jim Downs, coeditors of the series.

erupted with regularity. And no issue has seemed more pressing for southern historians than the issue of what to do about Confederate memorialization, as all American historians puzzle over the Civil War's mighty and multiple legacies.

Confederate memorialization was a major project by veterans' organizations, women's clubs, and civic movements within the former Confederate states particularly during the early decades of the twentieth century. The expansion of this movement was particularly dynamic for women. As Jacquelyn Dowd Hall explains, these groups were determined

> to assert women's cultural authority over virtually every representation of the region's past. [This they did] by lobbying for state archives and museums, national historic sites, and historic highways; compiling genealogies; interviewing former soldiers; writing history textbooks; and erecting monuments, which now moved triumphantly from cemeteries into town centers. More than half a century before women's history and public history emerged as fields of inquiry and action, the UDC, with other women's associations, strove to etch women's accomplishments into the historical record and to take history to the people, from the nursery and the fireside to the schoolhouse and the public square.[7]

This aggressive battle to retake public space was spearheaded by neo-Confederates and continues to be an ongoing struggle via flags and parades, all too familiar problem tools.[8] Disputes and debates over statuary in public spaces have taken center stage

---

7   Jacquelyn Dowd Hall, "'You Must Remember This': Autobiography as Social Critique," *Journal of American History* 85 (September 1998): 450.

8   For an interesting piece on Confederate flags and college dormitories. see Brooklyn Brown, "Confederate Flags in Dorm Rooms: What Students Think," *Teen Vogue*, 30 August 2017, https://www.teenvogue.com/story /confederate-flags-in-dorm-rooms.

in the past few years, as scholars and citizens, governments and voluntary organizations have clashed bitterly on the question of resolving historical conflicts through removal, relocation, or destruction.

Questions about legacy and legitimacy continue to bedevil. Most significantly, as the scholars in the following round table insist, statues and memorials tell us more about those who create these commemorations than they do about those being honored.

The pulling down of a Confederate statue by an angry crowd in Durham, North Carolina, on August 14, 2017 (captured on film), symbolized the growing frustration of many with the movement to reform and refashion public spaces.

The ongoing crisis on the Chapel Hill campus of the University of North Carolina over what to do with the statue of "Silent Sam," tumbled to the pavement by student protestors in August 2018, reflects the levels of conflict such matters evoke: clashes between authorities and protestors, faculty and administrators, alumni and campus community, and many more incendiary intersections.

History in the Headlines brought together a distinguished group of scholars to discuss not only the immediate issues of the day (November 10, 2017) but also how advocates of heritage might clash with best practices in history, how the role of public history shapes current historical sensibilities, and what scholars can do to respond to contemporary topics. A round table offers the possibility of both information and conversation, its informality an advantage to the casual reader. By bringing together diverse experiences and viewpoints, it provides a spirited discussion that allows for the free flow of opinion and a smorgasbord of suggestions.

All across America local governments are grappling with how to address Confederate statues. Most recent removals have not occurred in response to vandalism but have been voted on by state,

county, and city officials. To avoid protests by those opposing relocation, most removals have taken place unceremoniously in the
dead of night—well past midnight, often around 2:00 a.m.

Challenges to Confederate memorialization are long standing.
Even before the organization of the National Association for the
Advancement of Colored People (NAACP) in 1918, there were
movements to protest the revisionist agenda of neo-Confederate
forces at work in former rebel states—and around the nation generally. The glorification of Confederate partisans was only part of
the passion for women in bronze and marble men on horseback. In
addition to the preponderance of whites portrayed in celebratory
statuary, Civil War monuments sometimes featured persons of
African descent, most often portrayed in limited and stereotyped
roles. Beginning in 1997, with Kirk Savage's *Standing Soldiers,
Kneeling Slaves: Race, War and Monument in Nineteenth-Century
America* a steady stream of scholarship began challenging earlier
twentieth-century interpretations of Civil War figures, reevaluat-
ing such artistic representations as demeaning and racist.

Some investigators have gleaned crucial insight by examining
key aspects of memorialization campaigns, including failed attempts to erect statues. Tony Horwitz, for example, once explored
the 1923 case of white southern Congressmen suggesting that the
federal government fund a statue in the nation's capital "in memory of the faithful slave mammies of the South."[9] The suggestion
was in no way a *progressive* tribute to African Americans—as these
same politicians allowed a filibuster to defeat an antilynching bill.
African Americans raised strategic objections, and one black

9   Tony Horwitz, "The Mammy Washington Almost Had," *The Atlantic,*
    31 May 2013.

newspaper argued that instead of simply a Mammy, the statue of a "White Daddy" be included, showing a Mammy looking on helplessly while a young black woman was being assaulted. Several models were proposed, and an image of a Mammy with an infant at her breast (presumably white) won the contest.[10] But the massive outpouring of protest from African Americans derailed the memorial scheme, as Mary Church Terrell suggested prayer might ensure "lightning will strike it and the heavenly elements will send it crashing to the ground."[11] The statue never came to be, but the prospect of it mobilized a generation to agitate against such assaults.

Literature and popular culture cast Mammy as the inner core of a mountain of material producing, exporting, exploiting racism, and Foucault suggested we might dig deeper to excavate buried treasure.[12] Mammy as an instrument of racial hegemony provides a powerful undercurrent within scholarship that critiques Civil War–era nostalgia—demonstrating the potency of her presence. At the same time, the depiction of "bowing and scraping" black bondsmen—the valet, the coachman, the artisan, or the enslaved field-worker—equally demeaned black men in the literary canon. The demonization of black bodies after the Civil War was particularly damaging and effective propaganda—resulting in the "black beast" mythology that cast men of color as sexual deviants and potential rapists. The antidote to this racist trope was to introduce

10 Mammies are always depicted as old and overweight, contrary to all evidence that child minders were often young girls in the plantation household. See Catherine Clinton, *The Plantation Mistress: Woman's World in the Old South* (New York: Pantheon, 1982), 201–3.

11 Horwitz, "The Mammy Washington Almost Had."

12 Kimberly Wallace-Sanders, *Mammy: A Century of Race, Gender and Southern Memory* (Ann Arbor: University of Michigan Press, 2008), 3.

another, undermining the fear of African American males' physical prowess by emasculating black men by any means possible. White sculptors often decorated their compositions of Civil War figures with "kneeling" or supplicant African American males. Thus participants in the Black Lives Matter movement as well as other contemporary activists rightly resist white hegemony and intimidation—embodied in images of heroic Confederates, white supremacists, and the occasional black bondsman.

Dilemmas concerning Confederate statues and memorialization confront twenty-first-century scholars of the Civil War and the American South regularly—in their boardrooms, in their classrooms, in their communities. Media outlets frequently challenge historians to answer calls and field queries that present complex and contradictory elements. Often historians are asked only for sound bites, and increasingly scholars are training the next generation to prepare themselves for "elevator spiels": a succinct summation of the most riveting qualities of one's research in less than one hundred words. The dilemmas regarding memorialization posed to historians are increasingly tied to social policy and current affairs, challenges that must be met by today's politicians and citizens.

The round table of four distinguished scholars took place at the eighty-third meeting of the Southern Historical Association in Dallas, Texas, on November 10, 2017, less than three months after a deadly car attack in Charlottesville, Virginia, took the life of Heather Heyer, a young woman who was protesting racism in the wake of torchlight rallies opposing the removal of Confederate statuary. This escalation of violence and subsequent loss of life, this acute sense of confrontation, hung over us as we traversed a wide swath of territory.

During the round table, we explored not only the broad issue of statues and removal but larger questions regarding memorialization and historical responsibilities, raising as many other questions as answers. Historians, particularly those working on race and memory, or on citizenship and the Civil War, have been given unprecedented opportunity to testify to the connections between the past and present. As the agitation for social justice continues, scholars struggle to prompt it as well as to reflect.

Each voice that follows—whether it be in the comments and responses of the distinguished panel or in the editorials and speeches from respected and diverse scholars—affords a cascade of fascinating data and bracing debates. All the contributors try to offer creative insights and practical solutions to the conundrums such issues raise.

Our efforts are not meant as an intervention but as a contribution to the continuing dialogue on the important and incendiary topic of Confederate memorialization.

As long as historians connect their work to compelling dynamics, as long as scholars struggle to reveal layered truths not only for today's audience but for the readers of tomorrow, our work will thrive. Writers toggle between two goals: attempting to remain both relevant and above the fray. In an era of tweets and hashtags, we must be vigilant to get our own truths heard, lest those that are self-evident be forgotten.

Round Table
on Confederate Statues and Memorialization

November 10, 2017   *Dallas, Texas*

MODERATOR

Catherine Clinton holds the Denman Chair of American History at the University of Texas at San Antonio and is a professor emerita of Queen's University Belfast. She is the author or editor of more than twenty-five books. Her first book, *The Plantation Mistress: Woman's World in the Old South*, appeared in 1982, and her most recent, *Stepdaughters of History: Southern Women and the American Civil War* (2016), is based on her Fleming Lectures, delivered at Louisiana State University in 2012. She was a consultant for Steven Spielberg's *Lincoln* (2012), following publication of her biography, *Mrs. Lincoln: A Life* (2009). She is an elected member of the Society of American Historians and serves on the advisory board for Ford's Theatre, President Lincoln's Cottage at the Soldiers' Home, *Civil War Times*, and *Civil War History*. During 2016, she served as president of the Southern Historical Association and was awarded a Guggenheim Fellowship. She is currently working on a study of Union soldiers and insanity during and after the Civil War.

PANELISTS

W. Fitzhugh Brundage has been the William B. Umstead Distinguished Professor of History at the University of North Carolina at Chapel Hill since 2002. He has written on lynching, utopian socialism in the New South, white and black historical memory in the South since the Civil War, and African American participation in the creation of American popular culture. His most recent book traces debates about torture in the United States from the time of first European contact to the twenty-first century.

Karen L. Cox is a professor of history at the University of North Carolina at Charlotte. She is the author of three books and the coeditor of two others that examine southern history and culture. Her first book, *Dixie's Daughters: The United Daughters of the Confederacy and the Preservation of Confederate Culture*, has been given a second life following the events in Charlottesville, where white supremacists rallied on the premise of defending a monument to Robert E. Lee. She has emerged as a national and international expert on the subject of Confederate monuments and has written several op-eds for the *New York Times*, the *Washington Post*, and CNN. She's given numerous interviews about the monument issue to the BBC, *Newsweek*, *The Atlantic*, the *Los Angeles Times*, the *Wall Street Journal*, NPR, the *Daily Beast*, *Mic*, *Mother Jones*, and several other U.S. media outlets. She's also been interviewed about Confederate monuments for news articles in the leading papers of Ireland, Sweden, Denmark, Israel, Germany, France, and Japan.

Gary W. Gallagher, a native of Los Angeles, grew up in southern Colorado. He is the John L. Nau III Professor Emeritus of History at the University of Virginia. The author or editor of more than forty books, he has written about how the military and civilian spheres intersected during the Civil War, how the Civil War generation remembered the conflict, and how the mid-nineteenth-century crisis resonates in recent American culture.

Nell Irvin Painter is the author of seven books, most recently *The History of White People*, which made her a media expert on white people in the age of Trump. She is the Edwards Professor of American History Emerita at Princeton University, where she taught the history of the South. In June 2018, Counterpoint Press published *Old in Art School*, her memoir of BFA and MFA study in painting at an advanced age. She completed an artist's residency at the Brodsky Center printmaking studio in 2017.

CLINTON: To begin, I want each of you to recall your first contact with a Confederate statue or memorial and what your response was.

GALLAGHER: My first exposure to the Confederate memorial landscape was in the summer of 1965 when my mother and my grandmother and I drove from southern Colorado, where I lived, to battlefields in the East, and the first monuments I saw were in Vicksburg. We stopped where we crossed the Mississippi River, and I have a vivid memory. The one stuck in my mind was that of the sort of wild statue of Lloyd Tilghman[1] in Vicksburg.

---

1   The career of Brigadier General Lloyd Tilghman, born to a prominent Maryland family in 1816, pendulumed between military service, including a stint during the Mexican-American War, and civil engineering, building railroads in the United States and Panama. After Kentucky, his home since 1852, declared neutrality after the start of the Civil War, he joined the Confederate Army in Tennessee, commissioned as a colonel, and was later promoted to brigadier general. He surrendered

He seems to just be hit with an electric shock of some kind. And I took a picture of it with my Browning Brownie camera, which I had at the time. There is probably still a print floating around somewhere. I've been a hopeless Civil War buff since I was fourteen. It started when I was about nine, so for me the predominant feeling that I had was I am actually in a place where these things I've been reading about for so many years happened. There are not a lot of big Civil War battlefields in the southern part of the San Luis Valley in Colorado. That trip was the big "Here I am; this is where it actually happened." Obviously, I didn't attach any kind of political significance to it or have any notion of memory or anything like that. It was just, "There's Lloyd Tilghman, . . . and there's a statue of him."

CLINTON: Share who he was.

GALLAGHER: Lloyd Tilghman was a Confederate general. I'm sorry, we shouldn't assume anything. The Confederate general Lloyd Tilghman. It was the statue of him . . .

CLINTON: Was this a pilgrimage?

[Laughter]

GALLAGHER: A kind of third-tier general.

CLINTON: Was it your idea to go to Vicksburg? Or your family took you there?

GALLAGHER: Oh no, no . . . , we didn't have family vacations. I lived on a farm, and we didn't take any vacations, but my father let us go. We had twelve days, and we drove from Alamosa to Gettysburg and back in twelve days. I was allowed to go because

---

to Union forces at Fort Henry, Tennessee, where he was taken prisoner, then later released in a prisoner exchange. He resumed his command during the Vicksburg Campaign of 1863 and was killed in a battle at Champion Hill, Hinds County, Mississippi, on May 16, 1863.

I was in charge of irrigating our fields, and it's twelve days in between when we did that. My grandmother was the key. She bought me Civil War books when I was a little boy. She was the most wonderful influence. And so she kept a diary—I have her diary of the trip, which is really wonderful.

PAINTER: I grew up in California, so I didn't grow up with any Civil War memorials. Out west, in the Bay area, it was the Spanish past and the missions, though I always knew that the missions were kind of "iffy." I grew up in a left-wing household which was pan-African and attuned to the history of the American South. So, as far as Confederate memorials, I saw a whole bunch of them when I did dissertation research. I'm from California, and I love to drive. I drove all over. This was the early seventies, so you had to go to places, and I just drove all over the place in my VW Beetle—and with Massachusetts plates. And everybody said, "Aren't you afraid to go to the South with Massachusetts plates?" But I was fearless at that point. So I saw in my dissertation research all these sort of southern commemorations. And I thought, "Ugh, this is ancient history; it has nothing to do with me—all these crazy people." And I really didn't engage with them mentally. They were just part of a historical landscape. When I really started focusing was in the 1980s, when I taught at the University of North Carolina–Chapel Hill. And of course, there's a Confederate soldier . . .

GALLAGHER: Silent Sam.[2]

2 Given to the university in 1909 and placed in 1913, Silent Sam's inscriptions read, "Erected under the auspices of the North Carolina Division of the United Daughters of the Confederacy, aided by the alumni of the University," and "To the sons of the University who entered the war of 1861–65, in answer to the call of their country and whose lives taught the lesson of their great commander that

PAINTER: Silent Sam, yes. My sense of Silent Sam was that he was part of this local history which also had nothing to do with me. But I found it did kind of have something to do with me because, being from the Bay area and not being able to deal with heat and humidity, I also had to leave in the summer. So I would go to Maine in the summer and drive through Portland, Maine, which has a huge Union memorial. I would love to see that. I would just love to see that Union memorial, and it was like, "Ahh, I'm free" in the sense of free from the South of my everyday day-job life, and here I am in friendly territory. So that was my first real grappling with memorials of the Civil War.

But I should add that my husband and I did a semester in Berlin in 2001. We went to Berlin in part for *Vergangenheitsbewältigung*, or coming to terms with the past. Germans have been doing this very thoughtfully for a long time. I got involved with this field—with Germany being part of it—after [Daniel] Goldhagen's book *Hitler's Willing Executioners*. He got so much flack for that book. When it came out, we were actually in France, and maybe this was the French translation, but I read it, and I thought, "This needs to be done for American history." This was like in the nineties, when I first started thinking about coming to terms with the past, as historians were doing it, so from the nineties into the early part of the century. Then my book *The History of White People* [2010] appeared and was, in a way, this continuing engagement with the changing past.

BRUNDAGE: So the monument that I remember vividly as a child was a Confederate soldier monument in front of the old

duty is the sublimest word in the English language." Sam is silent because he carries no ammunition and cannot fire his gun.

courthouse in Leesburg, Virginia. My mother's family was from Leesburg, and part of my childhood I grew up there. My cousin and I particularly would play there a lot, but they had an interesting effect on me. I was actually born in Pennsylvania, and then growing up in Loudoun County, I was a Civil War buff from the age of six on. But I was a Pennsylvania Zouave.[3] My mother made a Pennsylvania Zouave outfit for me.

PAINTER: Oh, lovely.

BRUNDAGE: And I went to every battlefield, virtually every major battlefield of the South in my Pennsylvania Zouave outfit.

PAINTER: Terrific!

BRUNDAGE: And I even took pride in the first book I wrote. I was nine years old writing a novel about the Civil War which I still have . . .

GALLAGHER: What printing is it in?

[Laughter]

BRUNDAGE: Unfortunately, it's a private printing, but I love it. It has a preface, although I spelled preface "perface." And in the "perface," I say, "this is written from a northern point of view." So, in its own way, the monuments did not have the intended effect on me at all. But I have, I would say, the kind of childhood

---

3 The Pennsylvania Zouave uniform, worn most notably by the 114th Pennsylvania Volunteer Infantry Regiment, led by Charles H. T. Collis, who dubbed his initial company "Zouaves d'Afrique," consisted of red baggy pants, a dark blue collarless jacket with red Arabesque ornamental trim, a light blue sash, and white gaiters, and was worn alternately with a red fez or white turban. It emulated the uniform of the French light infantry first used in the French colonization of North Africa and made popular during the Crimean War. Although the uniform varied in color and detail, Zouave-clad military units fought on both sides of the American Civil War from more than thirty states but the uniform was most popular in New York and Pennsylvania.

nostalgia for that monument just in the sense that it was there. But I will tell you, there has never been a Confederate monument that moved me. It didn't have that effect on me.

GALLAGHER: Did you have a fez with your Zouave outfit?

BRUNDAGE: Unfortunately, my mother didn't know how to make one. But it was pretty good looking, I'll tell you. To see a nine-year-old running around on the battlefield with the flowing pants, with the piping—it was a good . . . it was a good look.

COX: Well, I don't have any childhood stories of a monument. I was born in West Virginia and our family relocated to Greensboro, North Carolina. I don't even recall confronting anything like this. So my first experiences with Confederate memorialization were in Fayetteville, North Carolina. I was a historian for the Museum of Cape Fear, and one of my colleagues was a woodworker, and he had salvaged wood and made things with them. He would make benches and make toys, or whatever, and he salvaged from the Confederate Woman's Home which was in Fayetteville, North Carolina. And he came to me and said, "I like to give a little history on, you know, where my benches come from, where the wood is salvaged from." Essentially, he asked me to research the home. That's what got me started on writing the book on the United Daughters of the Confederacy. I researched it. I went to where the Confederate Woman's Home was, which is actually kind of interesting. It was located next to Terry Sanford High School in Fayetteville. I saw this photograph of the day of the opening of this women's home, and there were hundreds of people there; all of these women were standing up in front, because they had been the ones driving this project and getting a state to take care of these women. And the state took over financing of the home, which they did until

1982. And so, the home had long been torn down, but there was still the cemetery where they buried the women who had been there, and it looked like a military cemetery. They had similar headstones that went throughout and so that was my first engagement with...

CLINTON: With a memorial.

COX: Yeah.

CLINTON: Statue or memorial?... was what I was asking about...

COX: Yeah, well the first one that I had been researching a long time was the Arlington Confederate Monument, which is a beautiful monument. You know, the United Daughters of the Confederacy...

GALLAGHER: The Moses Ezekiel monument.[4]

COX: Yeah, the Moses Ezekiel monument. The UDC hired the best artists for their work. They put bids out for designs, and artists from all over the country would bid on this. So for me, it was like I knew the narrative the monument offered was a southern narrative, a pro-Confederate narrative. But it was, it's still beautiful nonetheless. It's a piece of art and piece of sculpture for me. It was like, when I was an undergraduate and I was studying art history in a class and I got to the National Gallery and saw the Hudson River valley paintings for the first time. I was overwhelmed by it. And likewise, after having read about all the efforts to put this monument up and then seeing it for the first

---

4 The Confederate Memorial sits in Arlington National Cemetery, Virginia, and is titled "New South" by its designer, the noted Jewish American sculptor Moses Jacob Ezekiel, who fought for the Confederacy as a cadet at the Virginia Military Institute and is buried at the foot of its granite base. Unveiled in 1914, the thirty-two-foot-high bronze memorial was commissioned by the Arlington Confederate Memorial Association, which was led largely by members of the United Daughters of the Confederacy and the United Confederate Veterans.

time, seeing it, you know, the size of it and the scale of it, I had this similar feeling like I had been reading about this in school. Or, in this case, I had been researching it for a long time. And to see this in person was really impressive, even though I knew the darker history behind what was intended by those who put it up there.

CLINTON: Well, I sent out a few preliminary questions. So I'm really interested in asking about your sense that you are sometimes a historian or sometimes an observer in the world. And I'm interested in how these monuments can tell us about the past in different ways, in multilevel ways. I just participated in a symposium at the Speed Art Museum in Louisville where we talked about artistic representation. Indeed, we had artists there to talk about southern symbols amidst the controversy. But, just in reflection, does anyone have anything to contribute on the issue of artistic representation?

PAINTER: This is not so much artistic; it's more discourse. Actually, it was the year that I was president of the Southern Historical Association (2007). The meeting was in Richmond, and one of my former students was teaching there. He took my husband and me to the Jefferson Davis memorial, which is mostly, I mean, it's kind of anodyne pillars and such, but its text is the most tortured use of the English language that I have ever seen. That was what's really struck me.

CLINTON: How so?

PAINTER: It's full of "that which is's."

[Laughter]

PAINTER: These really convoluted sentences that to me were sort of anal retentive. I actually took pictures of the language because it was so remarkable and so uncomfortable.

GALLAGHER: Similar to the language in Stephens's Constitutional bill *View of the Late War between the States*, which is torture and very hard to work through.[5] Obviously, trying to change something that everybody knows was another way, but now we are going to pretend it's this way.

PAINTER: Yeah!

GALLAGHER: Virtually unreadable.

PAINTER: It is virtually unreadable and it's . . . so unreadable you think, "Oh, you know, he is hiding things. He is keeping secrets. He's also all tensed up." So you know, this is not visual art in that same way.

CLINTON: Right, right.

PAINTER: But I think the language is really revealing.

BRUNDAGE: I think the artistic representation extends widely from not only the "store-bought" monuments that were produced by northern foundries and shipped wherever, but also there were obelisks that drew upon cemetery artwork and funereal themes. If you didn't know the obelisk was a Confederate monument, you would think it was conventional cemetery art. The range of artistic expressions varies widely. But I think most people, when they think of a Confederate memorial, think of the common solider monument that stands in front of a courthouse as a genre. There are the exceptions, which may be grandiose like those for Lee and Jefferson Davis on Monument Avenue in Richmond, or it could be . . .

5   Alexander Hamilton Stephens (1812–83), vice president of the Confederate States, later member of the U.S. House of Representatives from Georgia and afterward governor of Georgia, gave the famous Cornerstone Speech, which defended slavery and praised white supremacy, a few weeks before the start of the Civil War.

CLINTON: An obelisk in St Louis.

BRUNDAGE: Yeah, or the Jefferson Davis Memorial in Kentucky that is gigantic.[6]

GALLAGHER: It's huge—three hundred feet.

BRUNDAGE: Yeah. Stone Mountain[7] being the extreme example: so imposing that you cannot help but recognize it and the other large monuments as artistic, as ambitiously aesthetic. But then, there are so many that are far less ambitious. So I just want to stress that it's important to acknowledge that many Confederate monuments are not Bernini sculptures.

COX: No.

CLINTON: No?

COX: No.

PAINTER: A friend of mine wrote a column in the [*New York*] *Times*, Sarah Lewis, an art historian. She wrote a column about the Confederate flag and the difficulty that Confederates had in agreeing on a flag that would project what they were about—which was about slavery—which they could also take abroad. So, you know, some people tried stuff with colors of people; white on the top and black on the bottom, things like that. And they realized that would not fly in, say, Europe. And so what

6 The Jefferson Davis State Historical Site was established near Davis's birthplace in Fairview, Kentucky. The monument is the tallest unreinforced concrete structure in the world. Completed in 1924, it is the second tallest obelisk in the world after the Washington Monument.

7 Stone Mountain Confederate Memorial is a rockface carving of Jefferson Davis, Robert E. Lee, and Thomas J. "Stonewall" Jackson that covers about three acres and is about four hundred feet above the ground. It was commissioned by the United Daughters of the Confederacy in 1915 and originally designed by Gutzon Borglum. Work on the project frequently stalled until it was redesigned and completed by Roy Faulkner in 1970.

they finally ended up with was a flag that was a battle flag, which kind of says, "Okay, this is a fight. This is all we can do." Because the goal of the Confederacy was unspeakable, or un . . . unpaintable, or un . . . unprintable in a sense.

CLINTON: At the art exhibit I was at [Southern Accent: Seeking the American Southern Contemporary Art, Speed Art Museum, April 30–October 14, 2017], the art of Sonya Clark showed viewers the actual surrender flag at Appomattox, which was made out of flour sacks. So fascinating because symbols have meanings depending on when you are looking at them, how you are looking at them.

GALLAGHER: But the Confederate flags are complicated because there was such an array of flags used. Different armies used different flags, and the one we think of as the Confederate flag, the one a lot of people call the Stars and Bars—the St. Andrews cross flag—that is not the Stars and Bars and was not the national flag. It wasn't used so widely in the Army in Tennessee and other places. I mean, we have all come to agree on what the Confederate flag is because of the ways it was used *after* the war. And that's really a postwar sense of what the flag was, how it was used and deployed, and by whom—after the war.

CLINTON: Well . . . that was my next question. What do these particular monuments and symbols reflect about the American Civil War versus what they reflect about the period in when they were erected. And, of course, I know, Fitz, you've done a lot of work on that recently and found a lot of surprises.

BRUNDAGE: Could you rephrase that again?

CLINTON: About your recent work on monuments . . . and when they were erected . . .

BRUNDAGE: Oh, okay.

CLINTON: This has been quite an opportunity, just the idea that it isn't always, you know, a Civil War monument. We as historians need to teach people it's also a monument reflecting the period in which it's erected.

COX: Well . . .

BRUNDAGE: Go ahead, Karen.

COX: I have written about it, so I often tell people that monuments are a reflection of the generation that got them built. It doesn't matter whether it's a World War II memorial or a Confederate monument. And certainly, there were some in the works before the Daughters of the Confederacy was founded in the 1890s. But from about the mid-1890s through World War I, when the vast majority were erected, it was a reflection of the values of that generation more than it was about the Confederacy. On the one hand, it was paying homage to their ancestors at some point. But it always came with a lot of ritual and ceremony and speeches that really identified what the monuments represented, which is why at the unveiling of Silent Sam, Julian Carr is talking about Anglo-Saxon supremacy. I was surprised to learn that, you know, even in Charlotte, North Carolina, in 1929, there was a reunion of veterans there. And during that time, they put up a monument that used language about these men as preservers of Anglo-Saxon supremacy, which is pretty late in monument building. Often the defenders of the monuments are saying we are erasing history if we remove these things. They need to ask themselves what history would be erased. No history is being erased. It's still going to be there. But they seem to have a disconnect between the period in which they were placed and the Civil War South.

GALLAGHER: I think it's important not to treat all monuments as being the same. I think a number of things that are written in the wake of Charlottesville[8] sort of flattens out the Confederate memorial landscape and treats them as if they are all the same—and they really are not the same. Women were so involved in the early memorialization . . . Using Charlottesville as an example, the earliest monument in Charlottesville is in the cemetery; it's on the university grounds, . . .

COX: Oh sure.

GALLAGHER: . . . Went up in 1893, and it was the ladies, the equivalent of a Ladies' Memorial Association—pre-UDC—who were the key people there. The tablets that were on the Rotunda at the University of Virginia and the one in front of the courthouse downtown were the same. It combines the things that Karen was talking about. They are sort of similar in some ways to the ones you see in little villages in England everywhere.

COX: Right.

GALLAGHER: I think the later ones in Charlottesville—the huge equestrian ones in Charlottesville of Jackson and Lee—I would put in a different class. And the Lee statue in Charlottesville went up in 1924. The speeches there were very similar in some ways to the comments made one year later in Congress when they decided to make Arlington the national memorial to R. E. Lee. This is part of a much broader stream. That same year the United States minted a half dollar with Lee and Jackson on it—1925, and Arlington was 1925. So I think it's important to put some of these monuments within the context of a much broader

---

8   A white supremacist "Unite the Right" rally to protest the removal of Confederate statues and a counterprotest in Charlottesville, Virginia, on August 12, 2017, turned into mob violence, which led to dozens injured and the death of thirty-two-year-old Heather Heyer, when a white nationalist drove his car into a crowd of counterprotestors.

phenomenon that was going on. Quite a different meaning in the early 1890s and right at the turn of the century.

COX: I agree with that. I think the monuments follow the phases of the Lost Cause, and so, in the initial phrases, there was really a lot about bereavement, and that's why those first monuments were in cemeteries.

GALLAGHER: Yes, yes.

CLINTON: And where to return them when they are removed becomes an interesting question. In San Antonio, in a large square, on top of a very tall obelisk was a soldier and the only text was "lest we forget."[9]

GALLAGHER: That is great . . .

[Laughter]

CLINTON: That monument also happened to be the only soldier monument that I know of so far that was designed by a woman. So a female artist created this . . .

GALLAGHER: Elisabet Ney[10] sculpted that incredible recumbent statue of Albert Sidney Johnston[11] in the state cemetery in Austin.

9   The Travis Park Confederate Monument was designed gratis by artist Virginia Montgomery of New Orleans. Her father served as a captain in the Confederate army, and her mother, who lived in San Antonio in the 1890s, was a member of the United Daughters of the Confederacy and reportedly suggested a statue of a common soldier, not a general.

10 Elisabet Ney, sculptor, born 1833 in Westphalia, Germany, educated in Munich, sculpted intellectual and political leaders throughout Europe until her marriage in 1863. After immigrating to the United States in 1871, her husband purchased a former plantation in Texas that she managed until 1892, when she opened an art studio in Austin, Texas, where she completed busts of Stephen F. Austin and Sam Houston, both housed in the state capitol, and the recumbent sculpture of Johnston, laid in 1905 over his grave in the state cemetery in Austin.

11 Albert Sidney Johnston, born in 1803 in Kentucky, owned a Texas plantation; served the Republic of Texas as adjutant general and secretary of war; the Texas

CLINTON: Yes, that's true.

GALLAGHER: It's very like the recumbent statue of Lee that Edward Valentine did in Lexington, Virginia, at Washington and Lee University.

CLINTON: Two Texas monuments designed by women. But in San Antonio, it's been removed at night by the city council, and I'm interested in finding out where it will end up. Returning it to a cemetery in our particular city is a problem because of where the Confederate cemetery is in relation to communities, etc. Gary brought up the point of flattening. So we as historians may, when we advocate for any number of solutions, see flattening as also a problem.

BRUNDAGE: Could I just jump back to the timing? There has been another boom in addition to the 1890–1930 boom, namely from 1990 to the present. If you look at the chronology of the Confederate monument construction, it wanes substantially during the 1940s, 1950s, 1960s, 1970s, but since 1990, the number of new monuments has gone up. And it has mainly gone up because of monuments erected at battlefields. And these new monuments have been erected by a combination of Civil War buffs and/or the Sons of Confederate Veterans.

CLINTON: So to what do you attribute the increase, as you're charting this?

BRUNDAGE: Right. I think it's important to recognize there are still Confederate monuments going up today. A few have been put up in public spaces other than Civil War battlefield sites. But

---

army as a brigadier general; and after Texas's annexation, the U.S. Army as a colonel during the Mexican-American War. In 1861, he resigned his U.S. Army commission to take command of the Western Department as a general in the Confederate army until his death at the Battle of Shiloh in 1862.

by erecting monuments on battlefields, the Sons of Confederate Veterans have found a safe ground. Within reason, you can put up almost anything on a battleground site, especially if it's a state battlefield.

GALLAGHER: It's not National Park Services.

BRUNDAGE: Yeah, if it's not National Park Services. Especially if the battlefield is a state site, and especially at an undeveloped state battlefield site, that they want to turn into a historic attraction. For example, Bentonville battlefield in North Carolina—very few people visit Bentonville, unless they're from nearby or they're driving up I-95 and want a break from the monotony.

GALLAGHER: Tell our readers where Bentonville is.

BRUNDAGE: Oh, Bentonville is in North Carolina.

PAINTER: Oh, North Carolina. I'm thinking Arkansas.

BRUNDAGE: Bentonville was a March 1865 battle in North Carolina that today is not heavily visited. Given that the site was underdeveloped up until the 1990s, park officials have obviously been quite eager to add monuments and develop the site. So the Sons of Confederate Veterans have been gradually erecting monuments there. It's a space where they can continue to give voice to their enthusiasm for the Confederacy, a space where they can do what they want with almost no oversight, no criticism, no politics involved. But their success speaks to the fact there is still energy in a small community to commemorate the Confederacy today.

GALLAGHER: I think powerful politicians play a role too. At Gettysburg and Mississippi, monuments have gone up—and there is a Maryland monument. If there is a member, especially in the Senate, who is interested in getting something done, even

in a place like Gettysburg, you can get it done. Normally, they
would not allow that.

PAINTER: You know, I'm going to add something to that, and I
am guessing here. I am just going to guess. The other day I was
sitting at the dinner table with my husband, who had gotten an
honor, and I said, "Oh, look, you're a shining star no matter who
you are." You remember that?

COX: Yes!

PAINTER: Earth, Wind, and Fire.

COX: Yeah!

PAINTER: So he had never heard of them, so I went and found
Earth, Wind, and Fire. I found it in 1970, and they did music
that was both pop music, rhythm and blues, jazz, everything.
And when I thought about that time, after civil rights, things
kind of calmed down, early seventies, very multicultural, very
Motown. We were getting all mixed up in the seventies, and so
I'm wondering—if, regarding Reagan and also "southern strategy"—now looking at the time we're in, we see this attempt to
put everybody back in his or her boxes. That was part of what
was going on post-Reagan—let's get everybody back in his or
her boxes. And it certainly happened with popular music. So
there's that crossover that was going on in the seventies with
Earth, Wind, and Fire and the Motown people. That was not
happening in the 1990s and early 2000s, so I think there's a cultural side to this as well, kind of meta, to reestablish order.

COX: Oh God, that's what I thought when I saw what went down
in Charlottesville. This is what it is about: even white supremacists knew this was a symbol of whiteness. And if you were to
read their manifesto, it is anti-immigrant, antifeminist, anti-
LGBT, anti- . . .

PAINTER: Anti-whatever. I bet they hate Earth, Wind, and Fire.

GALLAGHER: I bet they haven't heard of Earth, Wind, and Fire. That would be my guess.

CLINTON: I've been struck by teaching the Civil War now for years in Texas. I recently came across so many Texans, but also other contemporary country singers, who both compose and sing Civil War songs. I have been exposed to, for example, a song called "Dixieland" [by Steve Earle], and when someone approached me with it, I was . . . "uh-oh," but it was amazing. It's a story about an Irish immigrant who immigrates and ends up fighting against the Confederacy . . . in Dixie. A whole raft of songs emerged in the postcentenary era. And I'm also thinking about my poor darling little battlefield in Missouri, my home state, Wilson Creek, where they decided, "Let's build this up. Let's make this into something." Back to Fitz's point, about the mobilization for tourism. The twenty-first-century political agenda: maybe it's projecting a *tourist* agenda.

PAINTER: Uhumm.

CLINTON: Maybe it's projecting a "stop on the road."

GALLAGHER: In Charlottesville, the man who paid for the big statues in Charlottesville was named Paul Goodloe McIntire, and he put four big ones downtown, not just Lee and Jackson but also one of Lewis and Clark, with a kind of kneeling Sacagawea behind it, and also one of George Rogers Clark. They cluster around the heart of downtown and were kind of part of the city beautiful movement in the early 1920s. Also, I think they were about McIntire, who wanted to say, "Look what I did." And to come back to one of Karen's points about the women—the women are not involved in those four monuments. There is a gender difference in the way that some of this memorialization is done. The women are heavily involved in the early ones, the ones that are more about grieving . . .

COX: In the same period though, they were a driving force behind Stone Mountain and . . .

GALLAGHER: Oh no, no, no. I absolutely understand that, but both with the Ladies' Memorial Associations and then with UDC, there is a different kind of involvement with these equestrian statues. The men specially excluded women from the Lee statue movement in Richmond, for example.

COX: Well, that's a . . . that's a big switch because they needed the women's help fundraising to get . . .

GALLAGHER: Absolutely!

COX: To get the monuments up on Monument Avenue. Yeah, that is definitely a switch. I think also, too, by that time, the UDC had peaked. They felt like they may have an accomplished their goals.

GALLAGHER: What's the peak in membership for the UDC?

COX: I think it's World War I.

CLINTON: You know, Karen, I was shocked when I went there to work in their archives, in the seventies, to find out the average age of membership, at the time, was women in their forties.

COX: No, they were young.

CLINTON: But I remember thinking, "There's a new wave."

COX: They were young. People assumed they were aged women, but they weren't. They were young women. And so what you see is, you begin to see generational differences, and maybe that is where some of this gender difference in terms of who's putting up monuments. Or it's the money, or how they are doing this. Because for the longest time, they were complaining that men weren't helping them.

GALLAGHER: And they weren't helping them. That is why they were complaining.

COX: Exactly!

CLINTON: What about Texas, Gary? The problem in terms of the twenty-first-century response to the statuary at the University of Texas . . .

GALLAGHER: Sure.

CLINTON: And having the president [of the University of Texas Austin] say he took [it] down "for symmetry." I believe he was pressed on why he took down the statue of Woodrow Wilson as well as Jefferson Davis.

GALLAGHER: For balance because they—Wilson and Davis— flanked George Washington. They were there when I was a graduate student at the University of Texas in the seventies . . .

BRUNDAGE: Visual balance.

GALLAGHER: Yes, visual balance. Never mind that Lee was Woodrow Wilson's greatest hero, and he, Wilson, wrote a biography of him. Anyway, that was an issue into the midseventies, when I was a graduate student—what to do with statues on that part of the campus that runs away from the tower at Texas. And it has come up periodically over the years. Students sort of discover them every once in a while, and the issue flares up and then drops down. But this time it didn't.

BRUNDAGE: May I go back and make one more point.

CLINTON: Please.

BRUNDAGE: I think it's interesting that we are talking about Confederate memorializing, and there's no equivalent in Union memorialization to the role women play in Confederate memorialization. And . . .

COX: No, they had an organization—but it wasn't nearly as active.

GALLAGHER: And they had a United States government doing a lot of things. The women stepped in and did things... especially with the UDC. I mean there's a tremendous difference in that regard in terms of how memory and memorialization play out between the winners and the losers.

CLINTON: And a memorial to Elizabeth Thorn,[12] who buried the dead at Gettysburg, was only built in the last decade maybe?

GALLAGHER: Yes! And until then, there was only Jennie Wade[13] at Gettysburg.

BRUNDAGE: I think that's an important point because I think often most people don't see Union monuments unless they are looking for them. But the Confederate monuments are conspicuous because the Confederates lost, and yet they have monuments...

CLINTON: Do you think that's the major feature: being conspicuous, where they're placed?

BRUNDAGE: Well, just partially, but what I was going to say is white southerners knew they were losing the commemorative battle. Most people don't pay attention to the fact that Washington, D.C., is an enormous shrine to Union generals. There are big,

---

12 In July 1863, Elizabeth Thorn, mother of three and caretaker of the Gettysburg cemetery after her husband joined in the U.S. Army, buried 105 soldiers from the Battle of Gettysburg, with intermittent help, while six months pregnant. A seven-foot bronze statue of her, weary and pregnant, was created by Ron Tunison and dedicated in November 2002.

13 Mary Virginia "Jennie" Wade, also referred to as Ginnie, was the only civilian to die as a direct result of combat during the Battle of Gettysburg. After several bullets and an artillery shell struck her sister's home during the first two days of battle, the twenty-year-old white woman was struck by a stray bullet while baking bread or biscuits in the kitchen on July 3, 1863. A statue was placed on her grave in Evergreen cemetery in Gettysburg in 1900, and a statue of her, completed in 1984, sits in front of the home, now a museum, where she was killed.

beautiful, impressive monuments to Union generals all over
the city. If you stack up the Confederate memorials across the
South against Union memorials . . . and the Union cause always
has Augustus Saint-Gaudens's Fifty-Fourth Massachusetts monument in Boston, which trumps anything. The Confederate
monuments often pale by comparison. Many of the monuments
that were put up in the South, in terms of aesthetic significance
and power, are underwhelming. White southerners were in
an arms race with the North to create monuments to the Lost
Cause, and they were losing it, and they knew it. They talked
about that all the time. And then of course there was the rest
of American history as well that northerners were claiming as
their creation; Plymouth Rock, Boston and the Revolution, etc.
So white southerners were acutely aware of the competition to
control history, and that history was being written elsewhere by
other people.

CLINTON: They lost Thanksgiving.[14]

[Laughter]

GALLAGHER: And on Fitz's point about how the Union memorial landscape is really kind of invisible for most people: I love
to ask groups to whom I speak, "Where's Grant's memorial in
Washington?" They say, "Oh no, it's in New York." I say, "I'm
not talking about his tomb. Where is Grant's monument in
Washington?" Virtually no one knows. And it's this huge equestrian statue looking right down the mall.

---

14 Virginians claim the first Thanksgiving was held at Berkeley Plantation in
December 1619, and only after the Civil War could New England insist the
holiday was a Yankee invention, which was associated with Abraham Lincoln,
as he was the first president (since George Washington) to proclaim a national
Thanksgiving feast.

COX: Yeah.

GALLAGHER: It's in the place where you'd want to be. They don't even know it's there. They don't even know it's there.

BRUNDAGE: And they got off at Metro stops Farragut or McPherson.

GALLAGHER: They don't know . . .

BRUNDAGE: They're not even thinking these are Union generals. McClellan . . .

GALLAGHER: Even George B. McClellan[15] has an equestrian statue.

CLINTON: Isn't the equestrian statue the issue? Because again, I'm really struck by the first encounter with a monument. I'm thinking as a child, someone on horseback is just someone on horseback and who they were associated with comes later. Is that a possibility? And we're talking about the ways in which monuments strike us or . . . we don't recognize them. They're all over Washington. Of course, the Lincoln Memorial, you're dealing with . . .

COX: I don't know if you know about who created the Stonewall Jackson monument on horseback back in Manassas; it looks like he's been in the gym for six months.[16]

GALLAGHER: He's on steroids. He's Jackson . . . and his horse too.

COX: It's like he's all buff.

PAINTER: Is this the one where he's shooting?

15 George B. McClellan served as commander of the Army of the Potomac and general in chief in 1861 and 1862, until President Abraham Lincoln relieved him of duty, citing McClellan's unresponsiveness. In 1864, he ran as the Democratic presidential nominee against Lincoln and was defeated.

16 The statue of Thomas J. "Stonewall" Jackson in Manassas, Virginia, was designed by Italian-born sculptor Joseph Pollia and unveiled at its dedication on August 31, 1940.

COX: No, no.

GALLAGHER: No, he is like this. [Gesture, fist on hip]

COX: He looks like he's, you know, like an Arnold Schwarzenegger in his prime.

GALLAGHER: And so is his horse.

[Laughter]

COX: I want to reflect on what was said about this monument arms race. I remember that being a comment about Shiloh Battlefield and about how there had been all these monuments to Union soldiers. And the UDC in that area wanted to do something, and they couldn't put up the numbers, but they could raise enough money to build one big one that would outshine the rest. And so that's what they did. And that one is a kind of interesting, because it's a national landmark.

GALLAGHER: It's very interesting. They complained the same way at Gettysburg. Gettysburg has nearly fifteen hundred monuments, and the overwhelming majority are Union. Many regimentals, but the Confederate states put up their big monuments there, and the latest was . . . Mississippi and Alabama, Louisiana in the seventies.

CLINTON: Some of them are quite beautiful, aesthetically as well.

GALLAGHER: That Gutzon Borglum for North Carolina, it's an amazing monument.

CLINTON: So again, we are talking about the aesthetics of these things. Well, how do the Union monuments inform our debate today, or do they?

GALLAGHER: I don't think they do. You asked about first encounters with Confederate monuments. I encountered two Union monuments as a boy in Colorado—one in the state veterans' cemetery, where they had a Union soldier in the middle of the cemetery, and there is one in the plaza at Santa Fe which was put up in 1868. It's one of the very earliest Union monuments. It's an obelisk, and it talks to the defenders of the Union—put up by the legislature of the territory of New Mexico in 1866, '7, and '8, as it says on it.[17]

CLINTON: So we look at the way in which monuments can give us new insight by directing our attention . . . Yet you're a buff. But I think maybe most people do wander in to read inscriptions to get an idea. I'm saying the encounter . . .

GALLAGHER: This is a buff too. [Points to Brundage] I am not the only buff here.

[Laughter]

GALLAGHER: He was even younger than I was.

CLINTON: But if we could put on our historian hats for a minute and . . . can we think about how we conduct a conversation or a debate, particularly in a classroom or in a public forum where many of us have had to encounter hard, tough questioning? Are we able to talk about the advantages and disadvantages of the current state of controversy, in terms of removal, with a very highly charged debate going on? Certainly if government takes a position, as it has in many cities, and then conducts its business in the dark of night, you know, it speaks to a lot of controversial issues. So if we as historians are trying to inform people, can each of you think of a way in which to frame the debate pro and con? Is that a possibility?

PAINTER: Yeah, I was thinking about a conversation I had last night with historians, and these were young historians who had

17 The obelisk, located in Santa Fe, New Mexico, was dedicated in 1868 to soldiers who fought for the Union and in the Indian wars in New Mexico. The monument faced its own controversy over one inscription on its base that referred to "savage Indians." Someone chiseled away the adjective; it was never repaired.

gotten their PhDs at North Carolina, Chapel Hill. And one woman said that her activism was to take walking tours, and Catherine mentioned the *Stolpersteine*.[18] Those don't exist, and they should exist in the U.S. There should be a stone that makes you stumble and remember what is no longer there. We don't have that. But if you take people on a walking tour, which are prime tourist attractions, you can point out things. And something you said, Karen, which really struck me, which I had not thought of before, which was highlighting the *speeches* around the establishment of these monuments. That, I think, would be really useful.

CLINTON: If there's no monument there, then how does that conversation take place or that walking tour take place? Do you say, "This is the site of a former monument"?

PAINTER: Yeah, you say, "This is the site, and this is what people said."

CLINTON: Do you have a plaque? Again, because at one point the debate centered on replaquing or "countermonuments." I'm just going to confess that in print I have advocated for countermonuments. I thought effective ones might have been established. But I'm not going to talk about Confederate countermonuments right now, yet I am a big fan of Kara Walker.[19] I am going to say that I thought, just in the middle of all this, and again at the end of our conversation, I want to bring *Stolperstein* and

18 *Stolpersteine* are the stumbling stones placed around Germany and other countries where Nazis committed atrocities. The act of missing ones' footing, hence stumbling, reminds people of what awful things occurred at these particular places.

19 Kara Walker, an American contemporary painter, silhouettist, printmaker, installation artist, and filmmaker, explores race, gender, sexuality, violence, and identity in her work.

other issues into the debate. Recently statuary debates exploded over a bronze installation of a young girl with her arms akimbo being put up on Wall Street, facing down the gigantic stock market bronze bull that was there. And the bull, by the way, was just dropped onto the sidewalk by some group, not "authorized." And decades later the girl statue gets dropped in, and there's a dramatic "you take that statue out!" response by conservatives. So a good example of the debate over the politics of space. And I was trying to suggest at the beginning that people might respond to a horse statue which represents what happened *beyond* the Civil War? So if you remove it, do you get to have that discussion?

PAINTER: You have a stone there that says, "This is what was here." And you have a walking tour that says, "This is what they said when they put down what was here."

GALLAGHER: I've used the Charlottesville memorial landscape for twenty years. I've been at the University of Virginia for twenty years, and I've given walking tours going from the cemetery to the Rotunda to downtown, where the three statues cluster. And I read from the dedicatory speeches. There are wonderful ways to get at the difference between history and memory—for example, the inscriptions on the monuments. The one in the cemetery has the classic "fate denied them victory"—which is the great Lost Cause "we never could have won" argument. There it is, in a very succinct way. Of course, they didn't think that at the time. I find the monuments splendid teaching tools. We finish at the Lee monument, and there I point out it's not just Charlottesville doing this. This is going on in Washington; this is going on at the U.S. Mint and so forth. I found the landscape very useful.

CLINTON: And the landscape in Charlottesville, as I understand it, is intended to change with a new memorial being proposed.

GALLAGHER: Liz Varon and I have been pushing to have a monument . . . We've been doing research at the Nau Center at UVA. We found more than 250 black men from Albemarle County who fought in U.S. Colored Troops (USCT) units. The old number was zero, and the new number is 250. We think a monument in what's now called Emancipation Park, a memorial to the USCT men from Albemarle County, would make sense. So this would create a place where you could literally show how memory changes. The Lee statue is 1924, but this is whatever—2017. This is the Civil War and how it's played out. It has a lot of interpretive and explanatory potential. But we are a democracy, and if somebody votes to take them down, take them down.

COX: The headlines of my op-eds were like, you know, misleading about what I was really trying to say . . .

GALLAGHER: Karen, they actually were misleading. You didn't write the headlines.

COX: Right, I don't write the headlines. It was something like, "Why monuments must fall." I didn't write that. What I said was because these are all locally produced monuments that . . . the community is the place where those decisions should be made. A community evolves, and if the community decided that they wanted to remove it, then they should. I just said, "They had a moral responsibility to consider it."

GALLAGHER: There should be a process, though. Not just knocking it down.

COX: Exactly! A process. And so I was in Greenwood, Mississippi, and there was a woman who would take me around places, and we went to the Confederate monument there. And she told me a little about the history behind the monument and how locals had posed for some of the figures that are around the monument. And she said they had actually gotten together, a group of local citizens, to talk about what they want to do with it. Conversely, in the little Charlestown, West Virginia, where the six women who are descendants of slaves had petitioned to have this plaque removed from the courthouse which was put up in 1986, not...

GALLAGHER: *Eighty-six*?

COX: 1986, which was a rebuke of the Martin Luther King holiday. The head of the commission just shot the petitioners down. And they quote Trump, you know, that this is a slippery slope. What's going to be next? Even when a large number of the community came to the commission meeting, including a member of the United Daughters of the Confederacy, who was one of the members who helped put the plaque up, and was now asking for it to be removed. They shut it all down. And it was interesting to me...

PAINTER: Karen, who is "they"?

COX: The local commissioners in Charlestown, West Virginia— five white members. And so it's interesting to me that they put out this long explanation of their new ordinance that *nothing* can be removed, which is what states across the South are doing. And it's interesting to me how they adopt this language, then kind of flip it back on progressive people, and they say, "Well, we are a diverse community. We are against violence. We're against this and that. We don't want to do something that would create that scenario. So we are not going to take this down." But they wouldn't even listen to reason. Because it is West Virginia, let's create a memorial that says we honor *all* Civil War soldiers, and we also commemorate or acknowledge the enslaved community that was here. But they just shut it down.

CLINTON: So is the removal of Confederate statues an acknowledgment of the descendants of the enslaved in that particular community? Is it being removed in order to recognize emancipation, for example? Therefore, we as historians . . . let's pat ourselves on the back a bit for our pretty good job from the centenary to the sesquicentennial redefining the American Civil War as a war about slavery. If you studied the centenary and look at the politics of slavery, look at the politics of race, look at what happened in 1960–65 compared to the recent sesquicentennial, our current transformation challenges those Confederate memorials: memorialization established to rebuke the war's outcome, our national history. We are having a battle in textbooks. We're having a battle in flags. We're having referendums in states. We as historians are having an impact. Currently, we are being asked to moderate, to intervene. I'm sure every one of you has been asked to contribute to this debate. I'm trying to get at the issue that we as scholars are expected to argue pro and con. But when we are in the media spotlight, or when we are thrust into the headlines written for us, we often get, as Gary mentioned, flattened in a way: *we* are getting flattened. Can we do our jobs as historians in this climate?

BRUNDAGE: Can I just jump back to the question you posed just before this one? I think we need to avoid accepting the terms of the slippery-slope argument. We need to put the onus, so to speak, on those who insist that we maintain the landscape as it is. My argument is that the American commemorative landscape is 150 years old, more or less. It's a very *recent* creation. There were few monuments erected during the first half of the nineteenth century. Not until the late nineteenth century did

Americans begin erecting lots of monuments. As Americans, we should ask ourselves why any monument is sacred. Admittedly, the Lincoln Memorial, I would say, is sacred; nobody is going to touch that one. But obscure monuments in small towns? If people want to remove them: fine.

PAINTER: But there are the Sons of Confederacy people. That's their monument.

BRUNDAGE: Fine, and if they want to keep it . . .

PAINTER: And they do sometimes.

BRUNDAGE: But my point is the conversation should be about why we should keep any monument. What is the monument's cultural function at this moment in time? Is it advancing the identity we want for our community? Is it teaching the community what we want to have taught? Does it represent the values we embrace at this moment in time? Just because we inherited a monument doesn't mean we have to keep it. There is no obligation for us to preserve every monument we've inherited. In fact, we don't do it anyway. We don't do it now.

CLINTON: We as historians, usually are pretty sacred about destroying evidence . . .

BRUNDAGE: I'm not talking about destroying them. Public space is a valued commodity, and we, as a society, should have the choice to alter our public space, especially our most important civic spaces, to reflect who we are at any given moment. Of course, we should make any changes with a deliberate process. We should do it democratically, inclusively. But the onus should be on defenders of the current landscape to explain why the landscape we have now is the landscape we should have in fifty years, one hunded years. Let's not start with this assumption that the landscape we have now needs to be preserved as it is.

GALLAGHER: I agree with that. The process should decide whether you keep it or not. But if some group decided they're going to
keep one of these, I still think it's important, then, to balance it
with something else.

CLINTON: Beyond contexts? You need to understand when this
memorial was built and why it was built. You do the tour that
contextualizes it. But if it's standing there "lest we forget"—the
meaning of these monuments is not always as vague. We had
a group of German students who came in to talk at Trinity
University in San Antonio, and they were talking about their
memorials and monuments, and they were just so astonished:
"Well if these memorials don't suit the current taste, then take
them down." I mean, they were very matter of fact. One could
counter, "Really? You look at the art and label it 'degenerate'
and just take it down?" So, I'm trying to clarify—who commissions? Who determines? You were talking about democratic
process: what is that?

[Laughter]

CLINTON: Majority rules?

BRUNDAGE: Whatever community, the community itself should
decide. And I think, as a historian, I would feel obligated to defend the right of that community if it decides to keep the monument up. But then I also will feel obliged to encourage them to
interpret the monument broadly, fully, with complexity.

GALLAGHER: And maybe add another monument that would
bring some other part of this historic story to people.

CLINTON: So what is the need for monuments?

[Laughter]

GALLAGHER: Do we have fifteen seconds to answer?

[Laughter]

COX: I think it's to make the generation of people who put it there feel something. It's about them. It's . . .

CLINTON: Beyond funerary?

COX: Yeah.

PAINTER: I think it's about identity. I think it's related to people who want to obtain their DNAs so they can get their little genetic ancestry pie chart and feel like there is culture in their DNA. You know, Americans are such mongrels—hungry for clarification.

CLINTON: Within a twenty-first-century focus, no?

PAINTER: Yes, a sense of who am I? And who are we? And when I say "we" here, I mean just those right around us, you know, in our town, or in our county, or whoever is the group we want to identity with and make our rules.

CLINTON: Our community.

PAINTER: No, our polity, in a sense, whoever would make these decisions. And so it's real hard because in the towns you're talking about, there's a real controversy over who "we" is. But who are "we" in terms of governance? Who decides? But also, who "we" are in the sense of how history packs into our bodies and gives meaning to our bodies in a time and in a place. Can this be read backwards to give us an identity? Because we move around so much, you know, our kids are everywhere; our grandchildren are all mixed up. Who are we? For some, "Well, we have always been Confederates," or, "We have always been the children of slaves." For that matter, this kind of teleological thinking, of reading, our identity backwards, this happens to nonwhite people as well. I mean, think about black power. You would think that all African Americans had just gotten off the boat and are pure African in culture and in body, and there's no mixed-up Irish and German and Jewish and all the other stuff that goes into so many bodies of color. We are a mixed-up people, and I think this is a way of trying to make meaning, to clarify meaning in identity.

CLINTON: So recently, for example, a memorial was removed from the grounds of this Speed Art Museum, which is at the University of Louisville, and what happened to the memorial? Harrodsburg, Kentucky, took it. They moved it to another community. So on this question of removal, I think most of the removal movement is not dedicated to the principle of putting it in communities that are more conformable with it. But it is being removed because of the concept that it either triggers something offensive or is itself *offensive*. I think this is a larger debate: do you keep things within the landscape that make people uncomfortable?

COX: I'm willing to say, you know, particularly on the grounds of courthouses where citizens engage with their government or citizens have to go in, to be put on trial or whatever, that's very problematic.

CLINTON: So particular public space or all public space?

COX: No, no, on the grounds of courthouses or government property where citizens engage their government, whether it's local or state.

CLINTON: Okay, so if the government removes these symbolic impediments to justice or fairness or equality, then isn't the government being let off pretty easily in terms of its responsibilities?

PAINTER: No, because it's hard to do that.

CLINTON: It's hard to do that?

PAINTER: Even when the county or city council agrees, they do it in the dark of night . . . It's hard.

[All speaking at once]

COX: We have gotten to a place where states like North Carolina, Tennessee . . . what are the other ones, Georgia, Alabama . . .

BRUNDAGE: North Carolina.

COX: They have passed laws to prevent *any* removal. What they've done is taken away local control, which is kind of an ironic thing. Taking away the local control so they can't do anything, and they . . .

CLINTON: So with fracking—-so it goes with statues . . .

GALLAGHER: A counterargument to that is . . .

COX: I like counterarguments.

GALLAGHER: It's fun to argue different sides, but history is full of very unpleasant hard edges. And the idea that you can create spaces where no one will feel uneasy about anything is difficult to imagine—a landscape where *no one* is going to be upset about *anything*? In some instances I think you should have to confront unpleasant things about the past and deal with them. And that's another way in which I think these monuments can actually be useful. I think it is important where they are.

COX: Yeah.

GALLAGHER: The problem with the Confederate ones is that so many are right where you are talking about. They are right in front of the courthouses.

CLINTON: So if we put them in museums? Or would you put them in cemeteries?

COX: They are so huge. Some of them you can't put them in a museum!

GALLAGHER: The monuments in front on the capitol grounds in Texas, you'd have to be like the Air and Space Museum to have that.

CLINTON: Don't give Texans that challenge.

[Laughter]

GALLAGHER: I mean they are huge!

CLINTON: Fitz, when you were at the American Historical Association and we had a forum on this topic . . . were you the one who suggested the . . .

BRUNDAGE: The museum of white supremacy.

CLINTON: The museum of white supremacy.

BRUNDAGE: At Stone Mountain . . .

CLINTON: Or have a graveyard for . . .

[Laughter]

COX: Here's why it couldn't work—because the people, local communities, feel like they own them: that's mine. So these ideas of the parks where you can bring in . . .

CLINTON: We can segue into the fact that there are "memorial gardens" in Europe. I'm interested, again, in broadening the debate.

GALLAGHER: I was in a meeting with the National Park Service historians. Some people are saying: "Put the Confederate monuments in National Park sites. That's where they belong. Take them and put them on a battlefield." And the NPS response to that, and I agree with this, is, Why would you? They have nothing to do with a national battlefield. The reason they were put up, why they were put up may have nothing to do with that. Why does it make sense to put them on a national battlefield?

CLINTON: So he was in battle, and therefore, go put him on that battlefield. Fine.

[All speaking at once]

CLINTON: I'm just saying the basis for a statue is connected to the Civil War. Back to my initial issue: I'm struck by these memorials to war dead in individual states. For example, I see these beautiful funereal ones, and it's "tear that down" if it's to the Confederacy. We talked earlier about plaquing and contextualizing. If you give people the notion that, as Nell said, you want to remove it and put up the plaque explaining it, I'm just asking is there any advocacy for keeping the statues?

PAINTER: Sure.

CLINTON: And putting up a plaque? Do we have local commissions?

[All talking at once]

COX: That's why it's got to be a community's decision.

PAINTER: Yes.

GALLAGHER: I agree.

CLINTON: If the "community" decides . . . but aren't we dealing with local, state, as well as federal government?

PAINTER: Go vote.

GALLAGHER: In Charlottesville, the monument in front of the courthouse isn't actually in Charlottesville; it's in the county. So when the Charlottesville council discussed Lee and Jackson, they couldn't even talk about the one in front of the courthouse, even though it's only one hundred yards from the Stonewall Jackson equestrian statue. It's in a different . . .

PAINTER: Jurisdiction.

CLINTON: Well, mentioning Charlottesville and what went on there: a lot of the press reported that these rallies were local. I was there for earlier rallies, an earlier rendition. These were "outside people," and the idea they were mainly local was pretty ridiculous.

GALLAGHER: They weren't local. They came in from all over the place.

CLINTON: So you get invaded. You get invaded. The Battle of Bull Run Commemoration this year [2017] was cancelled because the police anticipated an invasion during a political rally scheduled to coincide with the [commemoration] . . . I believe in going and reinterpreting the Civil War but not under *actual* battle conditions. And we are all being put on guard that way. And you talked earlier about the tearing down of statues versus the removal of a statue. How do we deal with that now?

PAINTER: Well, I think *we* are not the people who make that decision. We are talking here, yes. This is the same week as the Virginia elections which made such a potent . . . I was going to say symbol, but it's not a symbol; it's a changing of power. When I said go vote . . . that is the answer to the question of what to do. Change. If the people in power are saying the wrong things or doing the wrong things, then vote them out. And I think that is going to be the answer to the kinds of decisions starting on the local level.

GALLAGHER: But the state law that Karen mentioned, that we've all mentioned—in Virginia—that's a state law passed by the legislators . . .

PAINTER: Yes, change the legislators.

GALLAGHER: Yes, they can change that law as well.

PAINTER: Yes.

COX: As gerrymandered as we are, I don't think we'll get . . .

CLINTON: I don't mean to cut this off, but I would at least like to shift, in the time we have left, to broadening this to talk more generally about memorials. If we look abroad and look at the way in which Europe, Africa, and Asia memorializes—we are in the middle of this great debate over Confederate memorials—but I'm very struck when in my "American Icons" class, we find complex situations. People regularly assault memorials. A Gandhi statue goes down in Ghana this year [2017]. You have debates across the world over colonial issues. There was a miniature Statue of Liberty put up in Hanoi before colonial wars of liberation—now gone! So you look at the way in which we are in a worldwide dilemma. How does the artistic community respond to the questions of memorial destruction, statue removal? In Europe, it was an artist who proposed raising stones on sidewalks or streets and on these stones putting the names of those who were removed, who were deported, who died during the Holocaust so that you are forced to encounter this historical landscape in your everyday life. Certainly, that has been proposed in terms of slavery memorials. I mean, twenty years ago, Toni Morrison said, "There is not a bench by the road, a tree scored, that really looks at this question of slavery." We now have a wonderful African American museum of history and culture in Washington, D.C. But we still are looking and talking about the historical landscape and memorials. African American soldier memorials is something you brought up, Gary, and I've seen them go up in towns where they have their Confederate and their Union memorials—a kind of stone or marble or bronze addendum.

GALLAGHER: They went up because of the kind of resurgence Fitz was talking about. I think they are a wonderful example of how popular culture can have an effect. The film *Glory*[20] had an enormous impact.

---

20 *Glory*, an American feature film starring Morgan Freeman, Denzel Washington, and Matthew Broderick, released in 1989, told the story of the Fifty-Fourth Regiment of the Massachusetts Volunteer Infantry, a regiment made up of free and formerly enslaved African Americans and white officers.

CLINTON: An African American soldier memorial was built in Washington, D.C.

GALLAGHER: Yes, I don't think that would've been built had *Glory* not come out. I really don't think it would have. And there's a monument to USCT men on the national battlefield at Petersburg. It went up in 1991, right after *Glory* came out. —it hadn't been there before—right where the USCT men fought. It's a very interesting kind of parallel. There's a statue of Robert E. Lee on horseback at Antietam that some private person put up. It's behind the Union lines—that really is kind of comical. The battle . . . it's really interesting how it continues to play out.

CLINTON: Memory battles abound, certainly the establishment of the Vietnam War Memorial and countermemorials put up or additional memorials. We can look at the way in which the recent debate over memorials to comfort women unfolded. There are quite a number of comfort women statues in the U.S., as well as in Korea.

GALLAGHER: My daughter-in-law is Japanese, and the history she got for World War II as a young woman—she's forty-six now—dealt with World War II by *not dealing* with World War II. They just kind of skip it, and then it's Hiroshima.

CLINTON: Most prominently, Germany and its history! They have really reformed their landscape.

PAINTER: Germany needed to reform the landscape in physical terms, but the theoretical underpinning comes from a historian named Pierre Nora in France. The French were talking about history and memory. What I'm hearing around this table is maybe the importance of what historians can do. What we're doing here can bring about other memorials. I'm not talking about other memorials in other parts of the world but other memorials here in the U.S. Part of the discussion of Confederate memorials includes the erection of the colored soldiers' memorials and so forth—or that plantation the *New York Times* wrote about . . .

COX: The Whitney Plantation.

CLINTON: Yes, which features a wall listing names of enslaved who came in by boat from the database done by Gwendolyn Midlo Hall. It's so powerful to see scholarship etched in stone.

PAINTER: I would say for me the importance coming out of this conversation is the need to broaden the conversation beyond Confederate memorials into memorials generally. How do we remember, say, the era of slavery in the Civil War and include all these other things as well so that we know that there are many alternatives?

BRUNDAGE: And I think another example is the truly fascinating debate going on in New York City about the J. Marion Sims monument right now. Sims was the "father of American gynecology."

PAINTER: Oh right, right.

BRUNDAGE: I think it's a very interesting conversation because of who is participating, especially feminists and women of color. What the monument is about—a medical pioneer who did some of his invasive medical research on enslaved and immigrant women—and how the monument is interpreted: is it a monument to a callous, bigoted surgeon who exploited powerless women or to a medical pioneer whose work improved the likelihood of women surviving childbirth? The question of what do you do with a historical figure whose contributions may be quite profound and yet deeply tainted.

GALLAGHER: Deeply tainted.

BRUNDAGE: So that's a classic instance where a monument is so much more than a simple monument to a historical figure and, instead, is a monument that invokes complex historical questions regarding misogyny, racism, bigotry, medical innovation, the scientific method of experimentation, etc., etc. We can hope that New York City is going to have a very thoughtful debate about how to deal with that monument.

CLINTON: I'm thinking also of the recent debate whereby the memorial which includes Albert Richard Parsons—a Haymarket victim who was hanged—has been under scrutiny. We look at his radicalism and look in Texas where he was advocating for the rights of emancipated slaves. Yet Parsons fought for the Confederacy as a young man. So therefore, we have a conundrum. Where do we draw the lines?

PAINTER: We're drawing the lines.

CLINTON: Well, the lines are being drawn all the time.

PAINTER: Let other people draw them. We don't have to.

[Laughter]

GALLAGHER: Well, the point Nell made is so hard to get students to understand, to really understand, the difference between history and memory.

COX: Oh yeah.

GALLAGHER: And these debates are some of the best tools we have to do that, to get them to understand historical complexity. This or that? Black or white? Which one is it? These kinds of things are very useful in conveying complexity, and the difference between history and memory.

CLINTON: So these contested moments can be some of the best examples. But we are also seeing outbreaks of violence and outbreaks of distortions of histories in the headlines in a way that is not just confusing our students but confounding public policy. I mean historians are so relevant and yet simultaneously history is being...

COX: It seems like everybody is a historian, you know. I supported the women petitioners in Charlestown by writing to the head of the commission and answered all those questions: Is this erasing history? Is this a "slippery slope"? And I documented everything, and the chair's response was that what I said was *idiotic*. He quoted President Trump about the monuments. So it's as if they don't even care. But somehow they are *better* historians and know better than anybody else.

GALLAGHER: Well, they have access to the Internet, and they'll say, "But I saw . . ." I was supposed to testify for fifteen minutes before the Charlottesville Commission—which was a well-put-together commission and very thoughtful—and ended up staying there two hours talking about all the things you just mentioned, Karen. Okay, what about this, what about that? And afterward, two of them came up, and I know I was talking and they were *there*, but they knew what they knew *before* I started to talk. And they *still* knew it when the discussion was over. It's because they have *their* sources, and their sources are just like ours because they saw it somewhere online. You can actually believe there were fifty thousand black Confederates soldiers involved if you look at certain things online. And you can even cite stuff, so it must be real.

BRUNDAGE: For all our talk about how historians have really transformed the understanding of the Civil War and slavery—which is absolutely true—we have to remember General [Michael] Kelly [White House chief of staff for Donald Trump in 2017] perhaps spoke for a generation when he made his comment that the Civil War could have been avoided if American politicians had just compromised. He probably read historians such as Roy F. Nichols and Avery Craven,[21] who saw the Civil War as the tragic result of northern abolitionist extremists and southern secessionist extremists tearing the nation apart.

GALLAGHER: And James G. Randall, that's where he got his Civil War.[22]

BRUNDAGE: The history Kelly probably learned . . . he was not misrepresenting what he had *learned in school*, but he apparently hasn't learned anything since.

GALLAGHER: He hadn't been reading since then.

BRUNDAGE: Exactly.

CLINTON: I may have been overstating it, but the notion that the war was about states' rights and not about slavery is something that continues to be debated, for example, in Texas schoolbooks.

COX: That's the interesting thing because I read something recently about this. We have a challenge because we can provide all this information as historians to them, but they believe what they want to believe. You can't change that.

PAINTER: You can vote and change the officeholders.

COX: I mean in terms of educating people, if they don't *want* to be educated—they decide, you know . . . It goes back to your point about identity. There is this feeling that removing monuments is removing something about who they are, something important

21 Roy F. Nichols (1896–1973), author of *The Stakes of Power, 1845–1877*, among other prominent U.S. histories, retired from the University of Pennsylvania. Avery Craven (1885–1980), scholar of the American South and author of *The Growth of Southern Nationalism, 1848–1861*, served on the faculty of the University of Chicago.

22 James G. Randall (1881–1953) was the author of *The Civil War and Reconstruction* (1937), which became a classic undergraduate textbook.

because of their heritage, that they're important because of that genealogy, and they think *that*'s what your destroying.

CLINTON: Is heritage divorced from history?

GALLAGHER: If they could see that slavery was really central to the coming of the Civil War, then somehow all of their heritage is tainted. All their ancestors are all monsters.

COX: Exactly.

GALLAGHER: So you're asking them basically to cut themselves loose from everybody in their past and agree that their past was awful.

COX: Yeah.

GALLAGHER: And that their people were awful.

COX: And that's what where we run up against a brick wall.

GALLAGHER: It's hard to get past that.

PAINTER: Vote them out.

COX: No, we are talking about just the regular folks.

PAINTER: No, that is the reality of the situation we are in, in a sharply divided country in which roughly 38–40 percent of people are, to use a shorthand, Trumpists. They are going to stay there. And the only way to change that . . . I mean you are not going to change their views. You have to change *who* represents them. And in situations where the majority are people who think like this, then there are other ways, when talking about maybe putting up a plaque next to or in addition to a monument or creating other ways of dealing with it. But fundamentally, we still live, God willing, in a democracy. If a question is fundamentally important, you change the answer by changing the officeholders.

GALLAGHER: And the question can always come up again and . . . I mean it's not forever when we decide something.

PAINTER: Yes.

BRUNDAGE: We mentioned popular culture previously. I'll use a musical example here. I don't want to exaggerate my optimism here, but on the other hand, I do think that there are generations of white southerners who are less invested in "southernness." We can see it manifest in popular culture in the "bro-country" of the last fifteen years. Brad Paisley [a West Virginia country-and-western singer] is a good example. He and some of the other country musicians are young, white men trying to navigate a world in which they're not adopting the hardline racial identities of the past. They are trying to navigate a world where they listen to hip-hop; they have black friends and move in a more biracial society than perhaps many before them did. They are trying to navigate a different way to a white southern identity. They may talk about the Confederate flag and things Confederate, but they are *not* anchoring their identity in that version of the South. There is a real possibility to have conversations about heritage with younger white southerners that may not be as fraught as such a conversation would have been in the past. Of course, there are going to be the white nationalists who show up in Charlottesville. There are going to be younger members of the Sons of the Confederate Veterans, but I don't think that the demographics are necessarily pointing to the perpetuation of neo-Confederates.

GALLAGHER: Even in Ryman Auditorium in Nashville, they took down the Confederate flag . . .

COX: They took that down?

GALLAGHER: It's gone. The Confederate's Veterans paid for the balcony there, and it was displayed across it, and then [it] went down this summer.

BRUNDAGE: Yeah, they won't publicize it. The CMA [Country Music Association] Awards are not going to have people denouncing the Confederacy. On the other hand, denouncers are going to anyways.

GALLAGHER: And they are.

CLINTON: And through popular culture, with movies having an influence and music having an influence, things change. When I first encountered a "South Shall Rise Again" T-shirt in my San Antonio classroom, I was alarmed—until I realized the slogan was above the Mexican flag! Context please!

BRUNDAGE: Right.

COX: I do want to point out something I saw in Charlotte, which was . . . I went to a Charlotte pride event and, you know, downtown . . .

CLINTON: A gay pride event.

COX: Yup, gay pride . . . and there was someone selling T-shirts that had the rainbow flag—but in the corner was the battle flag.

CLINTON: Of the Confederacy.

COX: Of the Confederacy. And then I'll see people who are just walking around, you know, that are pretty conservative. I mean they are at the gay pride festival, and they are wearing a battle flag on the back of their shirt.

PAINTER: Yup. Two separate things.

GALLAGHER: People are complicated.

COX: They are complicated!

COX: But I do agree with what Fitz said. I think there is this younger generation not as invested as some people are.

CLINTON: We also said that twenty years ago . . . and you know, is it because we teach memory differently?

PAINTER: It's a spiral, not a circle.

CLINTON: A spiral, not a circle.

PAINTER: So, where we were in the backlash, a post-Reagan backlash, is not the same as where we are in the post-Obama backlash. I mean it's a hard way to get anywhere, but things do change.

GALLAGHER: This can't go in the transcript, I'm sure, but Joan Waugh teaches at UCLA and teaches a Civil War class that had four hundred people in it. It was the second largest class in the department for years. And when she first proposed teaching it, they said, "Well, it doesn't fit our demographics," and they meant there are too many Asian American students at UCLA. Some people wondered whether Asian American students would care about the American Civil War. Well, the class was huge, and she told them one time she had eight Robert Lees in her class one semester. None related to the general!

[Laughter]

GALLAGHER: I do think it's changing. Of course, there's still a pretty significant residue, a sort of throwback attitude toward a lot of this, but they are on the losing side of this in the long term.

BRUNDAGE: Another thing that has been very striking about what has happened in the last three or four months is that the historical professional has been showcased to a degree that I can't remember in any other public controversy, showcased, if you will, to our great advantage.

GALLAGHER: They treat us as if they might actually want to hear what we have to say!

BRUNDAGE: Well, exactly. But if you think about the breadth of historians who participated in this conversation and the value added, I think the profession has definitely contributed. That, to me, is a surprising turn of events in the age of the internet . . .

CLINTON: But it is also the age of Twitter. It's also the age of people having Twitter handles, people doing blogs. When I was first teaching abroad, I was made aware of that in an international situation; I was instructed to go on Facebook to recruit international students. You have to reach people across the globe and highlight America and American studies. So during the past decade the History News Network is upping our game. Many places are making us realize that we need to speak out. That's why we have a new series called "History in the Headlines." These headlines, by the way, are going to be shaped by media and the media calling on us. The media interacting with historians is a relatively new phenomenon. You cannot respond to a media inquiry by saying: "I'll send you the manuscript of my next book." They want the . . .

BRUNDAGE: But the profession has responded. There has been an engagement by the profession which, as you say, is different than it might have been. It's not at the level it might have been during the Vietnam War era, but there is still a kind of engagement of academics . . .

CLINTON: What do you mean?

BRUNDAGE: Well, I mean, in a sense during the Vietnam War there was a level of some faculty being deeply, deeply engaged: teach-ins, etc., etc. It hasn't been quite that.

GALLAGHER: It has been at the University of Virginia since August.

BRUNDAGE: Right, but it hasn't been quite that level everywhere. Yet there is still a level of engagement—from what I sense— from the academy, which is very heartening.

CLINTON: Is it our responsibility as historians to *always* respond?

COX: It just depends. I mean, when I saw those guys in Charlottesville . . . something went off in me, like a switch. I was like, "I've got to write something." I just, you know, almost felt like a little bit of dread when I was talking to the editor of the [*New York*] *Times*. I just fully expected him to reach out, but I first reached out to him, and he said, "Let's just wait a day, just one day."

PAINTER: Is this Clay Risen?

COX: Uhumm. And so, I did it [wrote the piece] almost with a heavy heart, but I felt like I had to do it.

PAINTER: Really?

COX: Yeah.

CLINTON: Well some of us may have heavy hearts in other ways.

PAINTER: If somebody asked me, because you never know . . . but when I get asked to write, I write.

CLINTON: What about you, Gary?

GALLAGHER: I have no idea how many people I got asked by to comment. I actually don't trust most of the press, especially television, because they're not really seriously engaged. They don't really want to hear us. They really want us to say what they want us to say. And they want us to say that in forty-five seconds, and that's what they'll use! I just don't trust them. And so I did a few interviews. I did one on NPR, one on PBS; I did a few things and wrote just a couple of pieces.

CLINTON: And Katie Couric?

GALLAGHER: I did two good hours with Katie Couric, which might yield *six minutes* . . . Anyway, not worth it with most of them.

COX: Well, I think . . . I hear what you are saying because I know that it seems like . . .

GALLAGHER: And your *headlines* are part of the problem, Karen, that we talked about.

COX: *My* headlines? They're not "my" headlines.

GALLAGHER: No, no, you know what I mean. You write a thoughtful piece, and they slap a headline on it. And it's only the headline that people remember.

COX: It's true because I saw it repeated in foreign papers.

GALLAGHER: The headline?

COX: *Just* the headline! Which is not even what I said. But on the one hand, there were these really young production assistants calling me and asking, "Would you, like, give me a history of the United Daughters of the Confederacy?" And I spent years writing that book . . .

PAINTER: Yeah, but now you have an elevator speech on the Daughters of the Confederacy.

COX: But then . . .

GALLAGHER: They want the "this is my dissertation topic speech."

PAINTER: But you can do that. We *have* to do that.

CLINTON: So we are training a new generation of historians to do this?

COX: No. But I want to say there are online magazines like *Vice* and *Vox* and *Mic* that are reaching younger generations of people, and they wanted to know about it. I thought that was important to talk to them. And it was really well done, and it reaches thousands of millennials.

PAINTER: *Teen Vogue.*

COX: Yeah, anything.

CLINTON: Well, Karen, besides the headaches with headlines, you've talked about some of the follow-up that you get that doesn't encourage us to write . . .

GALLAGHER: I have a neo-Confederate hate mail file this thick [gestures a large gap] that I get from people.

COX: I save my hate email.

CLINTON: Well, won't it be a good archive?

BRUNDAGE: I got hate mail from, I'll call him an anarchist, an an-
tifa [militant leftist] because [of] the fact that I had created a
site for inventory of monuments. It is like, "Tear them all down,"
and I won't use the language they used but, "Tear them all down
and you are going to go rot in hell with them." So it's like "Hey,
I just count them, I didn't put them up."

CLINTON: We historians don't we tend to pick our subjects? They
don't pick us. So just on a final note, can we go around and have
each of you maybe give a comment on history and memory
—something which has come up a lot in 2017? What would you
each like to leave us with?

BRUNDAGE: We are in a debate not just in the American South
but also in the United States as a whole. And I think it's so welcome that we have a debate that extends literally from Hawaii
to Maine and, to a certain extent, far beyond Confederate
monuments. It should be monumental—concerning our commemorative identity and our commemorative landscape. We
should pursue history and memory as a kind of national reflection about our landscape. I would actually say Mayor Mitch
Landrieu and New Orleans should be our model as to how to
have that conversation. So in that regard, I would say it's tragic if
what happened in Charlottesville does not allow a wider discussion. But if we do have a wider discussion, it will be a welcome
moment for American history.

PAINTER: I have some things I wanted to say . . .

CLINTON: Please. . . .

PAINTER: One thing I would love for us to be able to do is broad-
cast the three words "history and memory"—just to get people
to understand that such concepts exist. It's crucially important.
The second thing is that when we talk about history and memory,

we need to talk about monuments related to the Confederacy, such as to the colored soldiers, so that it's not *only* about tearing down, and not only about *Confederate* monuments, but about related history and memory in the Civil War. That's the second thing. And the last thing, you started to ask about training graduate students and how professional historians should respond in this kind of climate. I would say, first of all, we have to do good, professional scholarly training. We expect our postgraduates to become academic historians. They have to have good scholarly bona fides. But in addition to their scholarly bona fides, they need an elevator speech about what they do and why it's important. They need to have *at least* two registers and probably three. Because the central register is talking to the [*New York*] *Times*, or talking to the [*Washington*] *Post*, in which you get 700 words—not just 50 or 250. So, think about the part that is 40,000 words. Think about the part that is 800 words, and think of the part that is 50 to 100 words.

CLINTON: And think about the Tweet.

PAINTER: 140 characters.

CLINTON: There you go.

GALLAGHER: I think this is a reminder, and I'll just follow up on what Fitz said. If all we do is talk to each other, it's a great way to make a living and we all love it. But in the end, we really do need to make an effort to bring or share the best of what our research and work yields. We can try to reach a broader audience because if we don't, it's really too much inside baseball, or remaining in our little treehouses—however you want to put it. It has to be more than just reaching only our own students. And in my lifetime, there have only been one or two opportunities equal to this one, where we are able to extend our reach. And in our field, we have an advantage that almost no *other* field in history has. In American history a Civil War remains so rich with opportunities, because so many of the issues from the war resonate now. They come straight down through the decades, and we are still talking about them.

COX: I just want to add that I think these kinds of events provided such a wonderful opportunity, for me, as a historian, to engage in this public conversation. It's important to see other historians engage and we don't always have to engage by writing op-eds for the *New York Times* or *Washington Post*. We can do it, though, at the *local* level and write for the local paper or our state paper about these issues. And I hope—-and I'm hopeful—that we'll use this moment. People are paying attention to this moment, and historians must use it to continue to influence decisions about other subjects—not just Confederate monuments. Whether it's mass incarceration or . . .

CLINTON: Sexual harassment . . .

COX: Yes! Exactly! Other issues of the day!

CLINTON: And I wanted to finish . . .

BRUNDAGE: Can I add one final thought?

CLINTON: Indeed.

BRUNDAGE: Well, I think this moment is so tied to the moment of Trump in so many different ways. In the last eight years, history enrollments at universities have declined across the country according to evidence gathered by the American Historical Association [AHA]. But I know from what Jim Grossman [executive director of the AHA] has said: history enrollments actually went *up* in the last year. I think there is a hunger, a history hunger. History *happened* last year in a way that surprised all of us. There is a kind of hunger to understand what just happened.

In its own way, I think this event fits into that issue as well . . . I'm not just saluting us as historians for having done a good job of engaging the pubic, but we have also been demonstrating the enduring value of history as a discipline. So, this is a moment when we are on display, and I think we have acquitted ourselves well. It is very important for us as a discipline going forward.

CLINTON: Well, I wanted to conclude by saying Jim Downs and I invited the four of you because you've been very disciplined at today's session—and also undisciplined enough to give so generously of your time to help us launch this project. We appreciate each of you for taking from your busy schedules because each of you has really been engaged in such a variety of projects. Nell, with your art and your forthcoming memoir [*Old in Art School: A Memoir of Starting Over*]. And Gary, wherever I go and whatever I'm doing, you've been there first leading the tours, leading the charges, a champion of the National Park Service, a force with which to be reckoned at the Nau Center at UVA, among other important initiatives. Fitz, you've really been marvelous, by showing us the way in which a project can actually change our views of *when* the memorials developed and how historical exploration of the landscape and excavation of the archives can reframe our arguments. Karen is out there with her blog [https://southinpopculture.com/] and books. So, this volume will, I hope, give us a lot to think about and inspire others.

PAINTER: And I hope it will have a Facebook page.

CLINTON: Surely, you jest.

PAINTER: No.

CLINTON: No, I'm saying, *of course*.

[Laughter]

CLINTON: And I think we will have some have wonderful photos,

and eventually podcasts, so it's been wonderful, a great morning, and thank you for everything. Thank you all so very much.
See you in the headlines!

Top Ten Articles

Many of the topics covered in the round table are highlighted in the opinion pieces that follow. The "top ten" selection herein is by no means scientific nor definitive. One of the best if not *the* best resource for readers to comprehend the full scope of issues with regard to Confederate statues remains the Southern Poverty Law Center report "Whose Heritage: Public Symbols of the Confederacy" (https://www.splcenter.org/20180604/whose-heritage-public-symbols-confederacy). Its riveting set of interactive data remains best viewed online and tops the book-ending bibliography, which is organized by category (websites, books, and articles) and by state. Because public opinion over Confederate memorials remains divided and continues to make headlines, the bibliography includes websites for Confederate heritage to allow for comparative perspective on the topic. The series website for History in the Headlines (www.ugapress.org/index.php/series/HIH) provides further materials to support this title and guides people to yet other resources.

The Mammy Washington Almost Had

TONY HORWITZ

The Atlantic, May 31, 2013

● Author Tony Horwitz chronicled the dramatic attempts by southern powerbrokers to assert their mastery through the establishment of a "Mammy monument" in the nation's capital in 1923. Although the statue was never completed, the debates over its design and significance illuminate the key conflicts that neo-Confederate ideology produced.

If I say the word "Mammy," you're likely to conjure up the character from *Gone With the Wind*. Or, you may think of Aunt Jemima, in her trademark kerchief, beaming from boxes of pancake mix.

What you probably won't picture is a massive slave woman, hewn from stone, cradling a white child atop a plinth in the nation's capital. Yet in 1923, the U.S. Senate authorized such a statue, "in memory of the faithful slave mammies of the South."

As a southern congressman stated in support of the monument: "The traveler, as he passes by, will recall that epoch of southern civilization" when "fidelity and loyalty" prevailed. "No class of any race of people held in bondage could be found anywhere who lived more free from care or distress."

Today, it seems incredible that Congress sanctioned a monument to so-called Faithful Slaves—just blocks from the Lincoln Memorial, which had been dedicated only months earlier. But the monument to the Great Emancipator masked the nation's retreat from the "new birth of freedom" Lincoln had called for at Gettysburg, three score and ten years before. By 1923, Jim Crow laws, rampant lynching, and economic peonage had effectively reenslaved blacks in the South. Blacks who migrated north during and after World War I were greeted by the worst race riots in the nation's history. In the capital, Virginia-born president Woodrow Wilson had recently segregated federal facilities and screened *Birth of a Nation* at the White House. The overtly racist movie exalted the Ku Klux Klan, which peaked at two million members in the 1920s and won control of mayors' offices and state legislatures across the land.

"We have this image of the 1920s as the Jazz Age, the birth of the modern, a world of skyscrapers and flappers," says David Blight, a Yale historian and leading scholar of race in the late nineteenth and early twentieth centuries. "But white supremacy had few better moments in our history."

The early 1900s were also the heyday of Old South nostalgia. Popular songs and best-selling novels depicted antebellum Dixie as a genteel land of benevolent "planters" and happy "servants." Central to this idyll was the figure of Mammy, who in popular imagination resembled Uncle Tom's wife, Aunt Chloe, a cheerful, plump slave in a checked kerchief. White performers blackened their faces to tell stories and sing spirituals in the style "of the old time 'house darkey.'" The ready-made pancake mix of Aunt Jemima—a "slave in a box," as one historian puts it—quickly became a national sensation; a "biography" of her was subtitled "the Most Famous Colored Woman in the World."

In reality, the pancake mix was the creation of two white men in Missouri, and they named it after a character in a minstrel song, not an actual slave cook. Similarly, there is more folklore than fact underlying the stereotype of matronly slaves nursing young whites. "I went in search of the mammy and couldn't find her," says historian Catherine Clinton, whose books include *Tara Revisited* and *Plantation Mistress*. "Most slaves who looked after white children were very young." In other words, more like Prissy in *Gone With the Wind* than Mammy.

Or even younger. Harriet Tubman, for instance, was seven when she began caring for a baby and was whipped if the infant cried. Ex-slaves interviewed by the WPA in the 1930s also told of nursing babies as girls themselves, while the older black women of Mammy lore looked after slave children whose mothers labored in the fields. These interviews also cast a harsh light on the supposedly privileged status of "house" slaves. One former slave recalled a "Mammy" being lashed "till de blood runned out"; another described a rape by the slaveowner's sons. "I can tell you that a white man laid a nigger gal whenever he wanted," said an ex-slave from Georgia who "went into the house as a waiting and nurse girl" between the ages of nine and twelve.

These and other routine cruelties didn't figure in the moonlight-and-magnolia romance that seized white imagination in the late nineteenth and early twentieth centuries. Nor was the Mammy craze of that era confined to literature, song, and marketing. It was fostered by groups such as the United Daughters of the Confederacy (UDC), which sought to recast the "Lost Cause" as a noble defense of a southern utopia. If slaves had been loyal, well treated, and content, it followed that emancipation and Reconstruction were calamitous—just as portrayed in *Birth of a Nation*. The ladies of the UDC honored aged blacks as "faithful Confederates" and even ghost-wrote testimonials such as "What Mammy Thinks of Freedom," in which an ex-slave says, "w'en I gits ter hebben, Lord, I hope I'll find its slabery."

This reactionary crusade culminated in a UDC campaign to build monuments to slaves who remained faithful out of "love of masters, mistresses and their children." Initially, this effort was confined to the South. But black migration to the North, race riots, and growing anxiety about what whites called the "Negro problem" made the nation more receptive to southern images of bygone racial order.

So did the ubiquity of nurturing Mammies in popular culture.

"Mammy was appealing at a particularly fraught time in national history," says Micki McElya, a historian at University of Connecticut and author of *Clinging to Mammy: The Faithful Slave in Twentieth-Century America*. "Mammy represents paternalism and affection between the races, a world where everyone understands their places."

This was certainly the message of Charles Stedman, a North Carolina congressman who in January 1923 introduced a Mammy monument bill on behalf of the Jefferson Davis Chapter of the UDC.

"They desired no change in their condition of life," Stedman said of the faithful slaves who would be honored. "The very few who are left look back at those days as the happy golden hours of their lives."

Stedman added that the bill "should find a responsive echo in the hearts of the citizens of this great Republic." It did, at least in the Senate, which voted for a land grant in the capital, so the UDC could erect the monument as "a gift to the people of the United States." The next day's *Washington Post* printed only a two-paragraph item, noting that the Senate had approved three monuments: to baseball, to a "former District commissioner," and to "faithful colored mammies."

African Americans, however, took far greater notice, led by the growing black press and by newly formed civil rights groups. "My own beloved mother was one of those unfortunates who had the flower of her youth spent in a slave cabin," one NAACP official wrote the *Washington Star*, describing the Mammy statue as "a symbol of our servitude to remind white and black alike that the menial callings are our place." He added: "If the South has such deep gratitude for the virtues of this devoted group from which it reaped vast riches, let it remove the numberless barriers it has gone out of its way to throw up against the progress" of blacks.

One such barrier was lynching, which claimed some twenty-five hundred lives between 1890 and 1920. The Senate, just weeks before approving the Mammy monument, had allowed a southern filibuster to defeat an antilynching bill. (One southern senator called it "a bill to encourage rape" by blacks, while another contrasted this menace with the "unspeakable love that every southern man feels for the old black nurse who took care of him in childhood.") The proximity of the lynching and Mammy debates prompted the *Chicago Defender* to publish a cartoon titled "Mockery," in which a southerner presents plans for the Mammy statue to the dangling body of a lynching victim. The *Baltimore Afro-American* offered its own vision of the planned monument: a frowning Mammy perched atop a washtub instead of a pedestal, her empty hand extended above the inscription: "In Grateful Memory to One We Never Paid a Cent of Wages During a Lifetime of Service."

Blacks also bristled at the stereotype of benignly affectionate relations between masters and hefty, aging Mammies, who seemed never to have families of their own. A truer monument, one paper suggested, would be a statue to a "White Daddy," sexually assaulting a young black woman as a Mammy looks helplessly on.

Plans for the actual UDC monument stoked still greater outrage.

One sculptor's model showed an Aunt Jemima–like figure holding a white child as two other children clung to her dress. These were "pickaninnies," the artist explained, "trying to have their mother pay attention to them instead of devoting all her time to the white children." Another sculptor proposed a seated Mammy with an infant at her breast, set within a columned fountain. The monument's backers favored this design and said it would be titled "The Fountain of Truth." According to the *Washington Post*, the monument was to be erected on Massachusetts Avenue, near an equestrian statue of the Union general Philip Sheridan.

But the monument bill had to pass a House committee before it could be enacted. And blacks not only fulminated against the statue; they organized protests. Petitions and letters poured into the offices of politicians and newspapers, including one presented by two thousand black women to Vice President Calvin Coolidge and the Speaker of the House. The women's auxiliary of the main Union veterans' organization, the Grand Army of the Republic, also condemned the monument as a "sickly sentimental proposition" and suggested the money would be better spent on "bettering conditions of the mammy's children."

Three months after the introduction of the monument bill in the Senate, Congress adjourned without having taken any further action. "Because of the controversy and resistance, it's ultimately allowed to die," says Micki McElya. And so, the Mammy statue quietly joined the ranks of monuments in the capital that were never built, including a towering "Mother's Memorial" and a plan for the Washington Monument that depicted the first president in a carriage atop thirty columns. The spot where Mammy was to have stood is now occupied by a statue of Tomas Garrigue Masaryk, a "champion of liberty" in Czechoslovakia.

But Mammy was by no means expunged from national consciousness. Four years after the monument proposal died, the first true "talkie," *The Jazz Singer*, featured a black-faced Al Jolson singing "Mammy." Twelve years later, Hattie McDaniel immortalized Mammy with her Oscar-winning performance in *Gone With the Wind*. In the 1950s and '60s, Disneyland included a restaurant called Aunt Jemima's Kitchen. And not until 1968 did Quaker Oats begin to give its famous cook a makeover; Jemima shed weight and her familiar bandana, gradually becoming the coiffed woman smiling from today's supermarket shelves.

Mammy also endures in stone, though not in the dramatic fashion the UDC once envisioned. At Confederate Park in Fort Mill, South Carolina, an obelisk "dedicated to the faithful slaves," unveiled in 1900, includes a Mammy cradling a baby. In 1914, a towering monument was unveiled at Arlington National Cemetery to the "Dead Heroes" of the Confederacy. Standing near the Tomb of the Unknown Soldier, the monument's frieze includes a turbaned and heavyset Mammy, holding up a white child for a departing rebel to embrace.

Today, at the nearby Lee Mansion, visitors get a truer glimpse of what a Mammy's life was like. Behind Robert E. Lee's stately columned home stand the simple slave quarters where up to ten people occupied a single room. In one, furnished with a pallet and chamber pot, lived "Nurse Judy," also known as "Mammy," who cared for Lee's children, one of whom described her in a letter as "very weak and thin."

Another counterpoint to the southern lore of contentedly servile black woman can be found across the Potomac River, at 10th and U Street in Northwest Washington. It is a monument titled "Spirit of Freedom," honoring the almost 210,000 blacks who served in the Union army and navy during the Civil War. The sculpture includes a black woman holding her own child, beside a black soldier. A monument to black servicemen was first proposed in 1916 but not built in Washington until 1998.

"I'm proud this country finally got around to honoring these guys who fought for freedom," says a recent visitor to the monument, Joseph Brown, a retired black finance manager from Houston. His pride, however, dimmed a bit when he was shown a grainy picture of the very different monument that was proposed in 1923. "You're kidding me. We almost put up Aunt Jemima near the Mall?"

Brown's grandmother worked in a white home in Louisiana. He believes many southerners were sincere in their affection for "Mammies" and "maids," noting that half the people at his grandmother's funeral were white. "That history really happened, and there was genuine closeness," he says. "But a Mammy monument? That's repugnant, because it's using her as a symbol of servitude."

Historian Catherine Clinton says that if the monument had been built, it would strike tourists today as "a monstrous apparition" from our past. It might even have been hidden from view, inside a box—the fate of a faithful slave memorial in Harpers Ferry, West Virginia. But rather than cringe over the Mammy monument, Clinton believes we should celebrate the "unsung heroism" of those who opposed it. The controversy mobilized black women whose protests were a precursor of their activism in the civil rights movement of later decades. One such pioneer was Mary Church Terrell, a daughter of slaves who became founding president of the National Association of Colored Women and later took part in pickets and other protests against segregation in the 1950s. As a leader of the protest against the Mammy monument, she warned that if it were built, thousands of blacks "will fervently pray that on some stormy night the lightning will strike it and the heavenly elements will send it crashing to the ground."

This wasn't necessary, Clinton observes, because Terrell and others "struck it down themselves."

More Than a Statue
Rethinking J. Marion Sims's Legacy

DEIRDRE COOPER OWENS

Rewire, August 24, 2017

● In this compelling reflection, Deirdre Cooper Owens weighs in with
personal testimony to demonstrate the way in which J. Gilmore Sims
might appear a relic of the past, and yet his legacy might live on within
the conflicts now being detected between white medical practitioners
and African American women patients. Cooper Owens suggests a more
nuanced appreciation of the role of this pioneering gynecologist whose
experiments reflected the racial insensitivities of his era.

A year ago in an Upper East Side Manhattan hospital room, I experienced the most intense physical pain of my life. I was beginning
my first phase of fertility treatments, and my endocrinologist was
dilating my cervix. He did not administer anesthesia during the
twenty-minute procedure.

Despite my agony, I could not help but be reminded of the
southern physician James Marion Sims and his fraught medical
legacy, especially as I was finishing my forthcoming book on the
history of American gynecology. I am a scholar who teaches and
writes about slavery, race, medicine, and the American origins of
gynecology. In my work, I cannot escape the looming shadow of

Sims—often called the "father of American gynecology"—within the history of medicine. Nor can I sidestep the conversations that surround Sims's early work on enslaved women. Over a five-year period of experimentation, he repaired their obstetrical fistulae, a chronic condition caused by childbirth and in which an abnormal opening between the bladder and vagina causes incontinence.

As I began my fertility journey, I was fully aware that Sims helped to pioneer fertility treatments in this country. I also recognized the irony of my situation: like Dr. Sims's enslaved women patients, I too had undergone a procedure without anesthesia that was to help me bear children.

During the past twenty years, Sims has emerged as a notorious figure in the history of medicine. Today, more than a hundred years after his death, his work and legacy are as relevant as ever. He, much like other slaveholding American "heroes," represents the United States' inconsistent and hypocritical relationship with democracy and freedom.

Modern-day critics are angry that J. Marion Sims operated on nearly a half-dozen enslaved women without the use of anesthesia. They are also are incensed that he has been so widely lauded in the Western world for his work in gynecology. Statues depict and honor him in New York's Central Park and the South Carolina Capitol in Columbia, and activists have demanded the removal of such memorials, even before recent protests about Confederate monuments. Hospitals in Dublin, Ireland, and in his home of Lancaster, South Carolina, bear his name. The lives of the enslaved women on whom he experimented—Anarcha, Betsy, and Lucy, among others—have been largely forgotten.

The controversy is twofold and tends to lack historical nuance. Sims has been painted as either a monstrous butcher or a benign figure who, despite his slaveowning status, wanted to cure all women from their distinctly gendered suffering. As a historian and researcher, I am usually frustrated by the ahistoricism and reductionism that have emerged on both sides of the Sims debate. To better understand Sims, his enslaved patients, and the state of medicine, we must contextualize the antebellum South and its racial politics.

Sims was a South Carolinian who grew up in a world where slavery and anti-black racism was normal. As a slave-owning physician, he practiced, as did so many of his peers, on sick black bodies for profit. Before Sims's most famous gynecological surgical work on Anarcha, Betsy, Lucy, and at least three other unidentified enslaved women, he examined and treated enslaved people with ailments that ranged from tetanus to cleft palate repair. In his medical writings and his memoir, Sims used patronizing and offensive language to describe his thoughts and treatment of women and black Americans. In this regard, just like in his experimental medical work, his views proved to be the norm and not the exception in his racial and gendered beliefs.

In my conversations during the last decade, I have had the most difficulty convincing others that Sims was not a deviant bent on mangling black women's reproductive organs. He followed a practice that medical doctors and schools established decades before he began his own work in gynecology.

As a slave owner, Dr. Sims was intimately aware of the economic value of having a healthy slave labor force. Maintaining black women's reproductive health was a major concern for slave owners. Medical colleges in southern urban enclaves like Charleston,

South Carolina, placed newspaper advertisements that sought out sick enslaved people to perform experimental medical surgeries and treatments. In order to gain access to enslaved people's bodies, medical professionals entered into legal contracts with slave owners. In these contractual agreements, doctors agreed to take on the financial costs of caring for sick slaves and promised not to intentionally harm enslaved patients during their hospitalization. Sims entered into such a contract with the owners of his enslaved experimental patients. It would not have been in his economic interest to physically harm his leased charges.

Throughout his career, Sims wrote about his disdain for anesthesia in surgical work. As a doctor, he privileged performing surgeries quickly so that the patient would not bleed to death. Toward the end of his career, he used anesthesia regularly because of the medical profession's acceptance of the practice, especially after the Civil War ended. Although he certainly believed that black women did not experience physical pain in the same ways that white women did, most white doctors ascribed to this ideology during the nineteenth century. The racial science and medicine of the day provided so-called conclusive evidence that black and white people were biologically distinct from each other and these differences were manifested in various ways.

Further, what is less known about Sims's experimental gynecological work on vesico-vaginal fistula is that he performed the same reparative surgical work on a poor Irish immigrant woman in New York, Mary Smith. He treated Smith as he did his enslaved patients. Sims did not anesthetize her during her operations and made her work in the hospital he founded, just as he made his enslaved patients work as his assistants during their experimental surgeries.

I have argued and continued to insist that James Marion Sims was a product of his time, but this fact does not detract from his role as a man who participated in a system that reduced human beings to moveable property, one that was built on violence, terror, and white supremacy. Yet, our assessments of him as a purveyor of racialized terror must include how historic figures were regarded by their peers. Sims noted in his memoir that the local white community and his two white medical apprentices abandoned him after two years of failed surgeries on his leased slave patients. Sims alluded in his autobiography that some of their criticisms stemmed from their concerns that he was more committed to building a reputation for himself than actually repairing these women's bodies. After he lost white support, he continued his experimental work on his enslaved patients in another way; he trained and made these women assist him in his slave hospital. His explicit treatment of them as reproductive laborers was informed by his status as a slave owner.

As a slave-owning physician, Sims did not believe in the humanity of his patients. He described black people as "niggers" in his writings and practiced a southern paternalism that was endemic of nearly every white man who lived during the time. His treatment of Mary Smith as a poor immigrant woman was just as problematic; he referred to her as a "loathsome creature."

Like the work of nearly every pioneering gynecological doctor who worked in the South during this time, his surgical work on enslaved women ultimately benefited all women. In fact, Sims's suture technique is still used by doctors today in fistula repair operations.

Yet, ethical issues linger. What are we to make of commemorative statues and honorific medical awards that provide uncritical praise of James Marion Sims as an uncomplicated hero? I support efforts to recontextualize the historical text on monuments to Sims. The names, statuses, and labor of his enslaved patients must always be linked to Sims because he would not have achieved success as the country's foremost gynecological surgeon without the institution of slavery and the forced availability of black women's bodies. His stature as a medical hero was built on the broken bodies of enslaved women. Just as "Founding Father" Thomas Jefferson's relationship to his slave concubine Sally Hemings has come under scrutiny and attack, so has Sims's legacy.

As a scholar who writes about the medical lives of enslaved women and slavery's enduring legacy for these women's descendants, I stress in my work and activism that we must continue to advocate for the end of health-care policies and practices that provide less than equitable care for black, poor, and immigrant women. How can we ensure that medical institutions, doctors, insurance companies, and pharmaceutical research companies do not continue to experiment and practice on black women's bodies unethically?

Too many communities of color have inherited the medical racism of Sims's era. Black women experience more invasive medical treatments in uterine fibroid treatment than white women and die in higher numbers in childbirth. Systemic racism requires that the fight for equality in medicine be rooted in the continued inclusion of medical humanities, a field that applies the humanities, social sciences, and the arts to medical education; in reforms in how biomedical ethics classes are taught in medical schools; and in legislation that does not harm women of color physically and legally.

Lastly, the legacy of medical racism affects us all despite our supposed social standing. The fact that I could be treated so callously in 2016 by a doctor who believed I did not need pain relief during my cervical dilation is a reminder that racism is ever-present in the medical field.

As recently as 2016, a University of Virginia study reported that some white medical professionals still believe there are biological differences between black and white people that shape their tolerance for pain. African Americans are thus often undertreated for pain.

My hope is that, while acknowledging how damaging racist symbols are for people of color who are reminded of the way "American heroes" achieved their status, we simultaneously work to eliminate racism within our educational and health-care systems at all levels. No medical doctor trained to heal women and their children should graduate with the same concepts about biological differences that Sims did in 1835.

Confederate Monuments and Tributes in the United States, Explained

SHELLEY PUHAK

Teen Vogue, September 6, 2017

● Shelley Puhak explores the vast number of controversial monuments dotting the American landscape. Her analysis of these statues and their critics shines a light on how young people today measure the current crisis over historical memorialization, particularly the fight to remove such statues. Although advertisements for articles on typical teen dilemmas may dot the online version of this piece, this op-ed nevertheless highlights how such topics can grab hold of the public imagination and enter into American youth culture today.

In recent weeks, public officials citing security concerns in the wake of violence in Charlottesville, Virginia, have hastily removed twelve statues dedicated to the Confederacy, including five in Maryland, two in Florida, and four in Texas. One more statue was pulled down by protesters in North Carolina and dozens more are slated for removal.

These are just some of the monuments lauding leaders and soldiers of the Confederate States of America, which was formed in 1861 when eleven states seceded from and then waged war against the United States to defend the institution of slavery. Calls to remove these monuments began in the 1990s and gained momentum after white supremacist Dylann Roof massacred nine African Americans in 2015.

The issue matters because monuments illustrate to citizens who is privileged in the public sphere. "To literally put the Confederacy on a pedestal in our most prominent places of honor is an inaccurate recitation of our full past, it is an affront to our present, and it is a bad prescription for our future," New Orleans's mayor Mitch Landrieu said earlier this year, explaining his city's decision to take down four such statues.

Critics argue that removing these monuments is, at best, a distraction, and, at worst, tampering with history. President Donald Trump opposes these actions, saying it was "sad to see the history and culture of our great country being ripped apart with the removal of our beautiful statues and monuments."

To better understand just how many of these monuments and statues are slated for removal, the *New York Times* has prepared an interactive map that shows how the landscape is changing. The Southern Poverty Law Center (SPLC) has created a comprehensive guide that details 1,503 monuments, including 718 (now 699) statues and monuments, that still exist on public property; it does *not* include more than 2,600 historical markers, museums, and other places or symbols that serve to explain—rather than honor—the history of the Confederacy, according to my calculations of SPLC data.

The data compiled by SPLC illuminates exactly whose history has been, and is still being, erased. According to the Smithsonian's Art Inventory database and my own calculations, the number of U.S. monuments honoring the Confederacy eclipse those U.S. monuments honoring any other cause or group of people in American history. For example, there are *seven times* as many statues honoring the Confederacy as there are statues lauding America's Founding Fathers, who get only around ninety, per my calculations of SPLC data. Confederate monuments aren't just in the South—they can be found in at least thirty-one states throughout the United States, including in states like Montana.

And they aren't all relics from the aftermath of the Civil War, either. In North Carolina, for example, thirty-five monuments have been added since 2000. And a new Confederate statue was recently erected in Alabama.

One Confederate general, Robert E. Lee—whose likeness was slated for removal in Charlottesville, drawing crowds of white nationalist protesters—is seen in six statues on public property in the United States, according to my calculations of SPLC data.

When added together, the total number of statues honoring two great civil rights leaders, Frederick Douglass and Dr. Martin Luther King Jr.—who each boast seven, according to my calculations from searching the Smithsonian's Art Inventory database—are still less than the nearly twenty statues erected to glorify Jefferson Davis, president of the Confederacy, according to the SPLC and my calculations.

If monuments typically honor the victorious, puzzlingly, there are twice as many U.S. military installations (ten) named after the generals who lost the Civil War as the Union military leaders who won it (five), according to my calculations. The SPLC notes that most were erected well after 1865, likely to reinforce Jim Crow laws or fight back against the civil rights movement.

For example, in 1964—almost a hundred years after the Civil War—discrimination against women and minorities was finally outlawed through a piece of landmark legislation. In the next five years, nearly thirty new monuments dedicated to the Confederacy were installed, according to my calculations of SPLC data. Less than ten were dedicated to those who fought for civil rights—and less than eighty exist, compared with the Confederacy's nearly fifteen hundred, according to my findings.

Public schools even pay homage to the fallen heroes of the South, with 109 named after Confederates, according to the SPLC. One-fourth of these schools have majority African American student population, meaning children attend schools named after people who fought against the literacy and freedom of black people. According to a search in the National Center for Education Statistics, more schools are named after Robert E. Lee (fifty-two) than after President Abraham Lincoln (forty-six), whose Emancipation Proclamation ended slavery in the United States.

According to the SPLC, Nathan Bedford Forrest—slave trader, war criminal, and grand wizard of the Ku Klux Klan—is the namesake of seven schools in the United States, while my search of the National Center for Education Statistics database shows only about five honor abolitionist Harriet Tubman.

In the United States, monuments to the Confederate States of America greatly outnumber those honoring this nation's founders, veterans, and activists, according to my calculations of SPLC data. And many have pointed out that these monuments exist in a vacuum, without mention of the victims of the institution the Confederacy defended. As Mayor Mitch Landrieu noted, "There are no slave ship monuments, no prominent markers on public land to remember the lynchings or the slave blocks. . . . So for those self-appointed defenders of history and the monuments, they are eerily silent on what amounts to this historical malfeasance, a lie by omission."

"The Civil War Lies on Us like a Sleeping Dragon"

America's Deadly Divide—and Why It Has Returned

DAVID BLIGHT

The Guardian, August 20, 2017

● In his pathbreaking work of memory studies, *Race and Reunion*, historian David Blight examined the impact of the nostalgia machines that cranked into gear during the decades following the Civil War. He postulates that the issues dividing the country in the middle decades of the nineteenth century persist in disuniting the nation today.

"I tremble for my country when I reflect that God is just," Thomas Jefferson wrote in 1781. The American revolution still raged, many of his own slaves had escaped, his beloved Virginia teetered on social and political chaos. Jefferson, who had crafted the Declaration of Independence for this fledgling nation at war with the world's strongest empire, felt deeply worried about whether his new country could survive with slavery, much less the war against Britain. Slavery was a system, said Jefferson, "daily exercised in tyranny," with slaveholders practicing "unremitting despotism," and the slaves a "degrading submission."

The founder was hopeless and hopeful. He admitted that slaveholding rendered his own class depraved "despots" and destroyed the "amor patriae" of their bondsmen. But his fear was universal. "Can the liberties of a nation be thought secure when we have removed their only firm basis, a conviction in the minds of the people that these liberties are of the gift of God?" This advocate of the natural rights tradition, and confounding contradictory genius, ended his rumination with the vague entreaty that his countrymen "be contented to hope" that a "mollifying" of the conditions of slaves and a new "spirit" from the Revolution would in the "order of events" save his country.

For that Republic to survive it took far more than hope and a faith in progress. Indeed, it did not survive; in roughly fourscore years it tore itself asunder over the issue of racial slavery, as well as over fateful contradictions in its constitution. The American disunion of 1861–65, the emancipation of four million slaves, and the reimagining of the second republic that resulted from the pivot of American history. The Civil War sits like the giant sleeping dragon of American history ever ready to rise up when we do not expect it and strike us with unbearable fire. It has happened here—existential civil war, fought with unspeakable death and suffering for fundamentally different visions of the future.

Republics are ever unsteady and at risk, as our first and second founders well understood. Americans love to believe their history is blessed and exceptional, the story of a people with creeds born of the Enlightenment that will govern the worst of human nature and inspire our "better angels" to hold us together. Sometimes they do. But this most diverse nation in the world is still an experiment, and we are once again in a political condition that has made us ask if we are on the verge of some kind of new civil conflict.

In one of his earliest speeches, the Young Men's Lyceum address, in 1838, Abraham Lincoln worried about politicians' unbridled ambition, about mob violence, and about the "perpetuation of our political institutions." The abolitionist Elijah Lovejoy had just been murdered by a mob the previous year in Illinois. Lincoln saw an "ill omen" across the land due to the slavery question. He felt a deep sense of responsibility inherited from the "fathers" of the Revolution. How to preserve and renew "the edifice of liberty and equal rights," he declared, provided the challenge of his generation. "At what point shall we expect the approach of danger?" Lincoln asked. "By what means shall we fortify against it?" His worries made him turn inward. "Shall we expect some transatlantic military giant to step the ocean, and crush us at a blow? Never! All the armies of Europe, Asia and Africa combined . . . could not by force, take a drink from the Ohio, or make a track on the Blue Ridge, in a trial of a thousand years." Lincoln did not fear foreign enemies. If "danger" would "ever reach us," he said, "it must spring up amongst us. It cannot come from abroad. If destruction be our lot, we must ourselves be its author and finisher. As a nation of free men, we must live through all time, or die by suicide."

Those words were prescient in Lincoln's own century. But they have a frightful clarity even today. Where are we now? Are Americans on the verge of some kind of social disintegration, political breakup, or collective nervous breakdown, as the writer Paul Starobin has recently asked? Starobin has written a new book, *Madness Rules the Hour: Charleston, 1860, and the Mania for War*, in which he revisits the old thesis that the secession moment represented a "crisis of fear" that led tragically to disunion and war. Psychologically and verbally, in the comment sections on the internet, and in talk-show television, we are a society, as Starobin shows, already engaged in a war of words. And it has been thus for a long time. Americans are expressing their hatreds, their deepest prejudices, and their fierce ideologies. It remains to be seen whether we have a deep enough well of tolerance and faith in free speech to endure this "catharsis" we seem to seek.

Psychological explanations, however, do not fully explain America's current political condition. We are in conflict about real and divergent ideas. Are we engaged, half-wittingly, in a slow suicide as a democracy? Are we engaged in a "cold civil war" as one writer has suggested? Or does it feel like 1859, as another expert wondered, with so much rhetorical and real violence in the air? The election, and performance in office of Donald Trump, have many serious people using words like "unprecedented," or phrases like "where in time are we" or "we haven't been here before." Commentators and ordinary citizens have been asking how or where in the past we can find parallels for our current condition.

For historians, Trump has been the gift that keeps on giving. His ignorance of American history, his flouting of political and constitutional traditions, his embrace of racist ideas and groups, his egregious uses of fear, his own party's moral bankruptcy in its inability to confront him, have forced the media to endlessly ask historians for help. That moral cowardice by Republicans shows some glimmers of hope; Mitt Romney has just called out Trump, accusing him of "unraveling . . . our national fabric" by his coziness with white supremacists, and Senator Bob Corker of Tennessee charged Trump with putting the nation "in great peril" by his incompetence and racism.

Sixteen years ago, in the book *Race and Reunion: The Civil War in American Memory*, I made a simple claim: "As long as America has a politics of race, it will have a politics of civil war memory." Unfortunately, despite many more fine books, as well as conferences and courses taught on the same subject, that prescription seems truer now than ever. The line from the killings of Travon Martin and Michael Brown, through a myriad of other police shootings, and then especially from the mass murder of nine African Americans in Charleston in June 2015 to the recent white supremacist demonstration and violence in Charlottesville mark a dizzying, crooked, but clear historical process. America is in the midst of yet another of its racial reckonings, which always confront us with a shock of events we are, pitifully, never collectively prepared for. Just now we are engaged in a frenzied wave of Confederate monument removals; it is a manifestation of how well-meaning Americans can demonstrate their antiracism and be full of admirable impulses. But this too in all likelihood will not itself prepare us for the next shock of events nor our next reckoning. Hence, we so achingly need to know more history.

All parallels are unsteady or untrustworthy. But the present is always embedded in the past. The 1850s, the fateful decade that led to the civil war, has many instructive lessons for us. Definitions of American nationalism, of just who was a true American, were in constant debate. After the Great Hunger in Ireland the United States experienced an unprecedented immigration wave between 1845 and the mid-1850s, prompting a rapid and powerful rise of nativism. Irish and German Catholics were unwelcome and worse. The Mexican-American war of 1846–48, the nation's first expansionist foreign conflict, stimulated an explosive political struggle over the expansion of slavery. The Fugitive Slave Act of 1850 caused a wave of "refugee" former slaves escaping the northern states into Canada, as well as a widespread crisis over violent rescues of fugitive slaves. Indeed, the constant flight of slaves from the South to free states was, in effect, America's first great refugee crisis. The abolition movement, the country's prototypical reform crusade, became increasingly politicized as it became more radical, extralegal, and violent.

At every turn in that decade, Americans had to ask whether their institutions would last. The two major political parties, the

Whigs and Democrats, either disintegrated or broke into sectional parts, North and South, over slavery. Third parties suddenly
emerged with success like no other time in our history. First the
Know-Nothings, or American Party, whose xenophobia and anti-
Catholicism got them elected in droves in New England in the early
1850s. And the most successful third party in our history, the
Republicans, were born in direct resistance to the Kansas-Nebraska
Act of 1854, championed by Democrats and which opened up the
western territories to the perpetual expansion of slavery. A succes-
sion of weak and pro-slavery presidents from 1844 through 1860
either tarnished the institution of the presidency or deepened the
sectional and partisan divide.

In 1857, the supreme court weighed in by declaring in *Dred
Scott v. Sandford* that blacks were not and could never be citizens of the United States. They had, wrote Chief Justice Roger
B Taney, "for more than a century been regarded as beings of an
inferior order . . . so far inferior that they had no rights which
the white man was bound to respect." This most notorious court
decision legally opened up all of the West, and for that matter,
all of the North to the presence of slavery. So discredited was
the Supreme Court among many northerners in the wake of the
decision that the Republicans made resistance to the judiciary
a rallying cry of their political insurgency. That impulse led to
the election of Lincoln in 1860, interpreted by most southern
slaveholders, who firmly controlled that region's politics, as the
primary impulse to secede from the Union. They believed they
could not coexist in a nation now led by a political organization
devoted to their destruction.

By the time of the sectionalized and polarized election of 1860,
conducted in a climate of violence and danger caused by John

Brown's raid on Harper's Ferry in 1859, North and South had developed broad-based mutual conspiracy theories of each other. They did so through a thriving and highly partisan press, in both daily and weekly newspapers. Both sides tended to have their own sets of facts and their own conceptions of both history and the Constitution.

White southerners feared and loathed abolitionists, and now they faced antislavery politicians who could truly affect power and legislation if elected. By the 1860 election, pro-slavery interests had developed a widespread theory about a "black Republican" conspiracy in the North, determined on taking hold of all reins of government to put slavery, as Lincoln in 1858 had actually said, on a "course of ultimate extinction." In the secession crisis, one southern leader after another pronounced against what they perceived as an abolitionist conspiracy against their livelihoods and their lives. William Harris, the secession commissioner for Mississippi, claimed in December 1860 that Republicans "now demand equality between the white and negro races, under our constitution; equality in representation, equality in the right of suffrage . . . equality in the social circle, equality in the rights of matrimony." He concluded, therefore, the Deep South faced a stark choice: "Sink or swim, live or die, survive or perish, the part of Mississippi is chosen, she will never submit to the principles and policy of this black Republican administration."

That Republican Party, along with radical abolitionists, advanced an equally potent idea of a "slave power" conspiracy that had grown into a staple of antislavery politics. The slave power, argued northerners, consisted of the southern slaveholding political class; they were obsessively bent on control of every level of government and every institution—presidency, courts, and Congress.

The slave power especially demanded control over future expansion of the United States in order for its system to survive. The theory made greater sense with time to many people, since they could see that the slave South, though wealthy, was increasingly a minority interest in the federal government.

No one made this case about the slave power better than the black abolitionist Frederick Douglass. In May 1853 Douglass gave the slave power clear definition. It was "a purely slavery party" in national affairs and its branches reached "far and wide in church and state." The conspiracy's "cardinal objects" were suppression of abolitionist speech, removal of free blacks from the United States, guarantees for slavery in the West, the "nationalization" of slavery in every state of the Union, and the expansion of slavery to Mexico and South America.

By 1855, as the Kansas crisis deepened, Douglass saw the slave power as an all-encompassing national plague with "instinctive rapacity," with a "natural craving after human flesh and blood." It was a "murderous onslaught" upon the rights of all Americans to sustain the claims of a few. Seeking consensus with the slave power, Douglass maintained, would be "thawing a deadly viper instead of killing it." He had faith in the "monster's" inherent tendency to overreach and destroy itself. "While crushing its millions," he said, "it is also crushing itself." It had "made such a frightful noise" with the "Fugitive Slave Act . . . the Nebraska bill, the recent marauding movements of the oligarchy in Kansas," that it now performed as the abolitionists' "most potent ally." Douglass detected a great change in northern public opinion. Instead of regarding the abolitionists as mere fanatics "crying wolf," the masses now perceived the evil in their midst and themselves cried "kill the wolf."

Thus we might see one of the strongest parallels of all between the road to disunion and our current predicament. The rhetoric about the slave power and about black Republicans has a familiar ring today. Millions of Americans on the right who garner their information from selective websites, radio shows, and Fox News possess all sorts of conspiratorial conceptions of liberals and the alleged radical views of professors on university campuses. Many on the left also know precious little about people in rural and sub-urban America who voted for Trump; coastal elites do sometimes hold contemptuous views bordering on the conspiratorial about the people they "fly over." Americans are more than politically polarized; we are bitterly divided about our expanding diversity, about the proper function of government, about the right to vote and how to protect it, over women's reproductive rights, about climate science, over whether we even believe in a social contract between citizens and the polity. In other words, as in the 1850s, we are divided over conflicting visions of our future. Let us hope that we find ways to fight out our current conflicts within politics and not between each other in our overarmed society. From my perspective, we can hope that like the slave power, the white supremacist far right will become its own worst enemy and, after all its frightful noise, kill itself.

As Americans consider the survival of their own amor patriae, we might reflect on just how old our story is. We love stories of exile and return, destruction and redemption. When Moses sent the Israelites across the Jordan, he instructed them to put up memory stones to mark their journey and their story. Americans have put up more than their share of memory stones and are just now living through a profound process of deciding which ones will remain. But as we look deeply into just what our own amor patriae means, and whether it can hold together, we might think hard about what inscriptions we want written on the memory stones of our own times. We might draw one from Douglass in 1867: "We ought to have our government so shaped that even when in the hands of a bad man we shall be safe."

Lincoln, Monuments, and Memory

HAROLD HOLZER

Civil War Times, November 21, 2017

● Lincoln scholar Harold Holzer has long been a champion of globalizing the local and connecting the local to the global. He has done much to champion seeing some statues not just as symbols of white supremacy but as works of art. Holzer delivered his remarks at the Gettysburg Cemetery, surrounded by statuary. During this, his own "Gettysburg Address," Holzer suggested we must judge these memorials as art as well as ideological projections.

Lincoln Prize–winning historian Harold Holzer, recipient of a 2008 National Humanities Medal, former cochairman of the U.S. Lincoln Bicentennial Commission, cochair of the Lincoln Forum, and *Civil War Times* Advisory Board member, delivered a speech at Gettysburg's Remembrance Day, November 19, 2017, celebrating the 154th anniversary of the Gettysburg Address and examining current monument issues.

His full remarks were as follows:

Some threescore and seven miles from this spot—in Washington—stands a statue of Abraham Lincoln. Not that one; another one: Thomas Ball's statue of Lincoln as a liberator, with one arm clutching the Emancipation Proclamation, the other extended in a blessing, lifting a shackled, half-naked African American from his knees.

It's unique because it was funded entirely by African American freedmen. Frederick Douglass himself dedicated it. "For the first time in history," he declared that day, people of color had "unveiled [and] set apart a monument of enduring bronze, in every feature of which the men of after-coming generations may read something of the exalted character and great works of Abraham Lincoln."

But today, Douglass's endorsement has been forgotten. The statue is out of fashion—politically incorrect. To some, the image of Lincoln looming above a kneeling slave is degrading. Critics believe it's time to take it down and erase it from both the cityscape and popular memory. Despite Douglass's hopes, it may not long endure, after all.

It is altogether fitting and proper to recall such contested sculpture here and now. We cannot reconsecrate this hallowed ground without acknowledging the statue controversy—the memory crisis—now roiling the country. We gather here above all to remember a great speech on a sacred spot. But Gettysburg is not only a final resting place for those who here gave their lives that the nation might live. It is an outdoor sculpture gallery too, with more than thirteen hundred monuments: Meade and Lee; Longstreet and Buford; Wadsworth and Warren.

These statues recall a time when valor, more than values, elevated subjects onto pedestals, and when, let's admit, the real issue that ignited secession and rebellion receded into the shadows; when the Lost Cause was still considered retrievable, and the words that Lincoln echoed here—that all men are created equal—remained a promise unfulfilled.

Now we are engaged in an often *un*civil war—a day of reckoning long coming—in which some historians have condemned, civic leaders removed, and activists have defaced, statues. Today, as we remember Lincoln and his finest hour, a speech that went on to inspire statues of its own, we face a challenge to countless other statues and to collective memory itself. Do we embrace it, revise it, or erase it?

The controversial Thomas Ball Lincoln recalls an age when Lincoln held the undisputed title of Great Emancipator. That was before African American agency and the U.S. colored Troops belatedly won recognition by whites as key instruments of black freedom. But does that overdue credit mean that all symbolic, if overzealous, tributes to Lincoln as the sole source of freedom should vanish, including one raised by African Americans them-selves? Such a purge could leave our history overcorrected and our landscape barren . . . and what Lincoln himself called his "greatest act" ignored.

Extremism on both ends of the historic pendulum can distort the arc of memory. Not enough, we must hope, to jeopardize Lincoln—still a hero in an unheroic age. But enough, I do hope, to make us recognize that the statues of Confederates erected in the South during Jim Crow are sincerely viewed by many as emblems not just of a lost cause, but a bad cause, a treacherous cause, and a racist cause.

The question is: should they come down? And if so, what hap-pens to the monuments here at Gettysburg, notwithstanding the National Park Service's recent vow to keep them safe for all time, because there are no forevers in the constant reappraisal of American memory.

Let's acknowledge one fact: this issue is far from new. Iconoclasm—the desire to destroy effigies—has been a part of the human experience ever since Moses destroyed the golden calf. The ancient Egyptians erased the memory of their only female pharaoh, Hatshepsut, by destroying her statues. Roman emperors obliterated the images of their predecessors. France tore down its Napoleon statues. And in both Canada and India, independence from the Commonwealth emboldened citizens to topple statues of Queen Victoria. But as good causes won, good art lost.

Nor have Americans been immune to such outbursts. In my own native New York, patriots celebrated the Declaration of Independence by hauling down a giant lead statue of King George III, breaking it to bits, and melting the fragments to make bullets to fight the British.

Lincoln iconoclasm has a history of its own. The U.S. Capitol rotunda boasts its own Lincoln-the-Emancipator statue. Never beloved, officials decided late in the nineteenth century to remove it. But in the process, workmen accidently broke off the Emancipation Proclamation that it holds in its hand. The workers promptly declared the mission jinxed and refused to carry it out. Instead of crating Lincoln up, they repaired the scroll and left it where it was. It has stood there ever since.

Yet consider this: on the other side of the world, where the public didn't have much to say about anything, not even the great Russian Revolution could purge the most famous monument in Leningrad: the giant equestrian of Peter the Great. The Communists simply embraced the legend that as long as the statue stood, the city would stand. Decades later, when the Nazis laid siege, the Soviets padded the bronze czar with sandbags and viewed its survival as the key to their own. It still stands today in the city again known as St. Petersburg. More recently, when the Taliban blew up the Bamiyan Buddhas, when Isis destroyed the ancient statues at Palmyra, people all over the world lamented these affronts to our shared culture, our common civilization. Which brings us to New

Orleans—Charlottesville—Memphis—Baltimore—and back to New York, where busts of Lee and Jackson have been exiled and statues of Christopher Columbus and Theodore Roosevelt face removal because of how they treated native peoples.

So what should we do about monuments that mark, even celebrate, what the Confederacy fought for, and the Union fought against? Statues do matter, because they compel us to look back, sometimes with pride, sometimes with anger. National ideals matter because they inspire us to look ahead. But without knowledge and care, emotions often rule—and irreversible decisions can be rushed by recrimination, the "fake news" of cultural reanalysis from a distance.

Still, we must acknowledge together that some statues are now touchstones for racists advocating their survival in the name of white supremacy, and we must summon the courage to condemn that impulse and disavow such rationales. That will give us standing to resist when other monuments, including Lincoln statues, become splatter boards for the red paint of misguided protest.

As some have. Recently, a Native American student organization conducted what it called a "die-in" before a Lincoln statue at the University of Wisconsin. The group's spokesman justified the protest this way: "Everyone thinks of Lincoln as the great freer of slaves, but let's be real. He owned slaves, and . . . ordered the execution of native men."

How can we deal with such views? Of course, Lincoln never owned slaves and did more than any man of his age to end it. Where this myth originated is baffling; that it continues to poison the internet is regrettable; that it percolates at the college level is nothing less than tragic; and that it informs the statue controversy is frightening.

As for the other charge: yes, Lincoln did authorize the execution of thirty-eight Sioux Indians in Minnesota convicted of rape and murder during the Dakota Uprising. But he pardoned three hundred others found guilty of only accompanying the others. Instead of a die-in at the Lincoln statue, why not a teach-in, or a plaque that explains the Sioux executions in full?

Defiling or dislodging statues reflexively—instead of reflectively—eradicates not only the original impulse for commemoration but knowledge of the events themselves. Is memory really worth obliterating—rather than comprehending and, where necessary, countering? Lincoln once said—not his most elegant phrase though he loved to repeat it: "Broken eggs can never be mended." Neither can broken statues. Might we here at least highly resolve to slow the rush to judgement—to consider the genuine benefit of art for art's sake, and to consider that wonderful alternative: context. Why not explain statues instead of reducing them to dust? Why not add new plaques or computer screens to tell full stories?

All of us should deeply sympathize with the many people sincerely offended by statues of Lee or Jackson and understandably resentful of having come of age in their shadow. Our Civil War past still haunts us. But obliterating relics cannot change yesterday; learning from them can change tomorrow.

Not all art is meant to fill us with joy. Think of the Arch of Titus in Rome, which glorifies the looting of the Jewish temple in Jerusalem, yet provokes no demands that it be torn down. As art, it deserves preservation; as history, it provokes discussion. Remember: statues can also be moved to museums, or cemeteries, or parks, or, yes, battlefields. In the South, if they stay where they are, the fate the Soviets chose for Peter the Great—with new plaques— they should testify to vanished and banished traditions—and not the vile efforts by postwar ideologues to perpetuate white heroes to intimidate black citizens.

But when we blow up memory altogether, and leave no trace of it for our children and theirs, we forget who we were, who we are, and how we can become something even better. Instead of leaving empty pedestals, why not raise high more monuments? Just as Richmond put up a statue of Arthur Ashe to face the Confederate leaders along Monument Avenue; just as Annapolis treated its disputed statue of Chief Justice Roger Taney, the man who ruled that black men could never be citizens. They did not tear it down. They raised up a statue of Thurgood Marshall, the first black man to sit on the Supreme Court, a supreme response, if ever there was one, to Taney's prejudice. What better way to trace the arc of American history than pointing first to Taney, and then to Marshall, to comprehend how far we've come, even if we still have a long way to go? Without Taney in place, Marshall stands at Annapolis without recognition of what he overcame. In New York, we just green-lit a new statue of Sojourner Truth—our first. And Central Park, which has 159 statues but only 2 of women—Alice in Wonderland and Mother Goose—will now get a real woman, Susan B. Anthony, to face nearby statues of Lincoln and Douglass.

Some statues are too misguided and offensive to survive. And they are bad artistically in the bargain. I count among these the tribute to the Battle of Liberty Place, the uprising against the mixed-race Reconstruction-era government of Louisiana. That monument was an outrage, and we should celebrate its removal by the mayor of New Orleans. Frankly, I have no love, either, for statues of Jefferson Davis, unpopular then, irredeemable now. But these are the exceptions, and I still hope they would not dictate the rule. Context, counterstatues, and relocation should always come first.

Let me end with one more proposal, an idea that acknowledges one of Gettysburg's living heroes, Professor Gabor Boritt. He was born in Budapest, a city that has been occupied, over time, by both Nazis and Communists. His own family fell victim to both rounds of terror. But even in Budapest, after decades of turmoil, Hungarians refused to destroy the public art once raised to celebrate villains. Instead, they created what they call "Memento Park." Here, old statues are arranged in a permanent display that, instead of erasing the painful memories of the past, compels people to confront, comprehend, remember, and above all, learn from them. Maybe we can be strong enough to do that here: to place the statues of disputed Civil War figures in memento parks of our own.

Lincoln once said, "We cannot escape history. We will be remembered in spite of ourselves." He posed for enough sculptors in his lifetime to suggest he profoundly understood the power of images to nourish that history. Let's not recoil from them. Let's use them as tools to learn from, and, when necessary, warn against. "Multiply his statues," Frederick Douglass said in dedicating the Thomas Ball Lincoln, "and let them endure forever."

Hopefully, we are now strong enough and wise enough, to preserve good art while condemning the bad impulses that inspired some of them. If not, we might suffer empty squares, empty parks, and, eventually, empty museums too. And maybe empty memories to go with them. Isn't it better to look than look away?

Let's take the time we need, so we can be sure, to paraphrase Lincoln, that we are honorable alike in what we give, what we preserve, and what we take away. Let's consider that even the most painful parts of our history should not perish from the earth, but long endure to be exposed and confronted.

Rather than defacing or dislodging these statues in anger, let's consider making some of them teachable instruments that illuminate neglected truths. Rather than take a sledgehammer to the unsettling past, let's fill in the gaps of our full national story. We have aside too much hallowed ground to stop remembering, and face too much unfinished work to stop striving to make the last, best hope of earth even better. In that spirit, may old statues inspire new statues, and may the monuments to a divided and divisive past yet become the foundations of a united future.

Confederate Memorials
Their Past and Futures

JANE TURNER CENSER

Washington, D.C., January 8, 2016

● Historian Jane Censer addressed the standing-room-only crowd of
historians at the American Historical Association annual meeting in
2016 to remind them of the origins of the Confederate memorial movement and southern white women's desire to preserve their past. Her
meditations on the memorial movement shine a light on the multiple
contexts that these statues and plaques represent.

Societies find different ways to remember the dead. But a way to acknowledge deaths in battle becomes particularly challenging when
those casualties fell in a war that ended in resounding defeat and the
end of the dream of separate nationhood. To be sure, the South had
never been united. Some white southerners had had doubts about
secession, but the outbreak of hostilities and a wartime mentality
silenced most of them as well as African Americans who, whether
enslaved or free, were not allowed a political voice. Still, Confederate
southerners were defeated in 1865, and they were reabsorbed into a
nation that for over four years they had reviled and demonized.

Thinking of the Civil War as a massive rupture raises questions
regarding early southern memorials for wartime dead as well as

questions of how we should deal, all these years later, with the symbols and memorials of that rebellion. The words we use indicate some of that ambiguity. Commemorate in its various definitions means "to call to remembrance," "to mark by a ceremony or observance," or "serve as a memorial." And memorialize too has that quality of bringing about remembrance. These terms differ somewhat and were less problematic to the victors than "honoring" and "celebrating." Postwar white southerners employed both kinds of symbols—those that commemorated and those that celebrated—as in fact Confederate memorialization changed over time.

This evening I want to discuss some of the memorial efforts undertaken after the Civil War, most of them by southern white women. These efforts in part rose in reaction to the government in Washington, which was overseeing the creation of national cemeteries that held only Union soldiers, white and African American. Beginning late in 1865 white southern women created Ladies Memorial Associations (LMAs) in towns and cities. Women started such a society in Winchester, Virginia, after a farmer plowing his field, uncovered bones of soldiers; by the spring of 1866 they had solicited gifts amounting to $250 toward "removing and suitably interring" the Confederate dead "scattered throughout the Valley." Similarly, the Appomattox ladies organization declared its purpose "to provide suitable interment for the Confederate soldiers who came to their end by battle or decease in this part of the country, whose bodies have not been deposited in some regular burying-ground."

Many of the women forming Ladies Memorial Associations had been involved in soldier aid societies and hospitals, and they cared deeply about what we might call civic housekeeping that would bring order and tranquility to a landscape where the dead were still quite untidily present. The Ladies Memorial Associations were best known for their Decoration Days, a chosen day varying among different towns and cities when much of the white community would march to the cemetery and decorate graves. Some Ladies Memorial Associations, however, such as those of Petersburg, Raleigh, and Richmond, became deeply involved in long-term programs of finding, identifying, and moving the remains of soldiers. Much like the efforts in the North to move deceased Union soldiers from areas near battlefields to national cemeteries, the Raleigh and Richmond societies not only reburied corpses and bones from the nearby countryside but also over many years paid for shipping bodies from the Gettysburg area.

To be sure, the ladies did not do the actual physical labor of shipping and reinterring the bodies, but they oversaw the necessary financial transactions. In 1866 in Petersburg, Virginia, women moved bodies and erected headboards. The Raleigh group did the same, over time replacing their deteriorating headboards with stones. Such groups also raised money to set up memorial statuary in the cemeteries. Rather than depictions of soldiers, these first memorials tended to be arches, obelisks, or triangles.

At this time white southerners argued that the ladies' efforts were apolitical—women at the natural womanly work of mourning. Yet, of course these actions had political facets, since the women clearly saw themselves as fulfilling patriotic duties, even if the object of their patriotism no longer existed. And even as the women's associations prepared the cemeteries and oversaw annual decoration days, other commemorative efforts in the white community were taking place. From the beginning, some southern whites wanted a more celebratory approach to their Civil War past. Historian William Blair has pointed out various activities that only thinly disguised a martial tone, as when militia companies in their old gray uniforms (with all military insignias removed according to law) marched in Decoration Day activities in Richmond.

After white southerners took control of state governments in the 1870s, veterans assumed a greater role in commemorative events. With the women's cooperation the Confederate veteran organizations unleashed a tide of commemorative statues—some equestrian, others of common soldiers—that swept through the South. By the late 1880s southern efforts to remember had changed from gathering the dead in cemeteries and giving each an individual headstone to glorifying the dead heroes of the Confederacy. The founding of the United Daughters of the Confederacy in 1895, as well as the greater activity of veteran organizations, gave rise to even more activities and new honorific ones. Gaines Foster and Fitz Brundage have chronicled well how, after the 1880s, Confederate memorialization moved from the cemetery to the courthouse square or similar prominent locales. White southerners showed their power by dominating public space with martial monuments—the Confederate soldier guarding the city or the Confederate officer on his valiant steed. Almost from its inception the Daughters of the Confederacy took a more confrontational tone than the LMAs had assumed. To be sure, some Ladies Memorial societies still existed and still focused on cemeteries, but the UDC was far more popular and more active. From efforts to depict slavery as a kind and gentle institution and secession as hinging on constitutional questions, the Daughters assumed what Karen Cox, their modern historian, has called a role of "vindication" that glorified the rightness of the Lost Cause—and crusaded for a white supremacist point of view. And UDC members in partnership with the veterans left their mark upon the land in many places. Indeed, in 1914 they succeeded in placing a memorial to the Confederacy on the grounds of Arlington National Cemetery as a gift to the United States.

And even though I as a historian am far more comfortable dealing with nineteenth-century people than twenty-first-century policy, I suggest that knowledge of the way these Confederate statues came to exist can offer something to our decisions about statues and symbols. Few people today give much thought to these cemeteries that mark and mourn the individuals who fell in the Civil War, and I suspect that even fewer would want to enter cemeteries and make significant changes. *Purpose matters.* Even though cemeteries generally are not closed to the public, they are not "public" in the same way as parks, city squares, schools, and other governmental buildings. These latter monuments to Jefferson Davis and so many of the Confederate military and political leaders are monuments of glorification—built in an attempt to vindicate, not just remember, the southern war for a separate slaveholding nation.

Should we move or discard such symbols as monuments that extol a group of people who sought to dissolve the United States? This is a difficult question. I find many monuments to the leaders of the Confederacy to be celebratory in a divisive manner; perhaps as a first step we should start with those symbols whose purpose from their establishment was most clearly to celebrate disunion and white supremacy. Moving some of these past symbols and memorials to the cemeteries of the nineteenth century or the museums of the twenty-first seems to me to offer a way forward.

Empty Pedestals
What Should Be Done with Civic Monuments
to the Confederacy and Its Leaders?

Civil War Times, October 2017

● Distinguished scholars on the scholarly advisory board of the *Civil War Times Magazine*, one of the leading popular journals in the field, with a subscriber list that reaches a far wider audience than an equivalent academic journal, chime in with their solutions for how to resolve the problems surrounding removal of Confederate statues. With suggestions varying from total destruction to preservation as public art with modification of signage, historians from different backgrounds contribute detailed and considered opinions on how to deal with current battles over bronze and marble.

From Charlottesville, Virginia, to New Orleans, Louisiana, the removal of Confederate statues from public spaces and the debates over their removal are making national news. Numerous other southern communities, large and small, are reconsidering the future of the southern soldiers in marble and bronze that stand watch over their town squares and courthouses. What will be their fates? As a bimonthly magazine, *Civil War Times* has a hard time being newsworthy and current. Often news stories that occur when we are putting an issue together will be "cold" by the time that issue is completed and sent off to the printer. The monument controversy, however, appears to be one that will remain topical for some time, and I feel that *CWT* needs to address the debate in some manner as it grows in intensity. I think it would be interesting, timely, and important for readers to hear views on monument removal. So to that end, I asked members of the magazine's advisory board, all highly respected scholars and authors, as well as some other selected authorities, to send us their opinions on Confederate monument removal. Their interesting and thoughtful answers are diverse, and some are likely to be controversial. The removal of Confederate monuments is a complex issue.—Dana B. Shoaf

JAMES J. BROOMALL
Director
George Tyler Moore Center for the Study of the Civil War
Shepherd University

I am an academic historian who practices public history and advocates for preservation. The removal of Confederate monuments troubles me as much as the destruction of a historic building or the total "rehabilitation" of a battlefield. The built environment contains countless lessons if allowed to speak. Make no mistake, the bronze sentinels and stone plinths found primarily in southern cities and towns offer an incomplete, even dangerous message if they remain silent. I can therefore appreciate why so many people wish for their removal. Confederate monuments are at once symbols of white supremacy, works of art, affirmations of the Lost Cause, and tributes to white southerners. Yet, public history and preservation suggest that Confederate monuments can be used as tools for education, deliberation, and even protest. Interpretive signage and additional memorials or statuary offer one way to convey the thick historical and aesthetic layers associated with these relics. We can further democratize these spaces by capturing oral histories of the current monument debates, advocating teach-ins and dramatic performances, or encouraging viewers to create temporary discursive signage. Confederate monuments remind audiences of a painful past but can also give voice to contemporary social concerns and needs if they are allowed to speak.

CATHERINE CLINTON
Denman Chair of American History
University of Texas–San Antonio

Headlines frequently call for the removal of Confederate monuments. Scholars try to learn from case to case how we can help communities find a place to debate how the culture of Confederate veneration affects the lives of those who live in the shadow of pro-slavery symbols.

Many suggest that eradication of these public symbols will create safe spaces and rescue the hostility felt by those resentful of Confederate remnants. What if monuments today might become more creative? In Germany, artists install "stoperstein," stumbling blocks on the pavement adorned with names and dates of Holocaust victims. These arresting public installations remind passersby of those led to their deaths by a monstrous and unjust government.

Americans witnessed a controversy over a 2016 "Fearless Girl" statue installation in lower Manhattan. Public art can raise hackles, as well as awareness of critical issues. Perhaps we would be better served by funding countermonuments to feed the hunger for new and different stories told with imagination. Perhaps shared spaces can become places where conflicting interpretations of circumstances might be highlighted.

Static nineteenth- and twentieth-century visions set in stone might seem objectionable, but it's probably equally offensive to try to sanitize the past without a plan to feed the human desire for knowing what's come before in order to understand what might lie ahead.

CHRISTY S. COLEMAN
CEO
American Civil War Museum
Richmond, Virginia

In the past two years, the American Civil War Museum has fielded numerous calls regarding controversies about Confederate imagery. Many want the museum to take a firm stand to support or oppose the removal of these items from the public landscape. As an organization, we rely on our mission to guide our actions.

In short, ACWM is a resource for communities to explore the war and its legacies. We recently hosted a symposium called Lightning Rods for Controversy (aired by C-SPAN) to frame the conversation and give interested parties the opportunity to hear from content experts. In addition, our unmatched archival and artifact collections contain important documents and information to help address the "who, what, where, when, and—most important—why," these monuments and symbols were placed. When communities are armed with this information, we are hopeful they will make well-informed decisions with reasoned discourse with all stakeholders.

At the heart of these discussions and debates is the core question of how we choose to remember. When it comes to the American

Civil War, the answer is not always "blue and gray." Americans of every background grapple with the war's legacies in contemporary times. This history is not dead or past. This history is our present.

WILLIAM C. DAVIS
Professor of History, retired
Virginia Tech University

In the passionate debate over where—and whether—the Confederacy merits remembrance today, we forget that changing values and demographics have always imperiled past generations' heroes. Nowhere is it written that heroes remain in place for all posterity. Where are the statues of George III today? New times make new heroes. Before 1968 there were no Martin Luther King Boulevards; today there are hundreds.

Removing statues in New Orleans and elsewhere is unfortunate, however understandable. Occasionally circumstances demand change. Nathan Bedford Forrest High School in Jacksonville, Florida, was all white in 1959. By 2014 it had a substantial black student population. African Americans attending a school honoring a slave dealer (and possible abettor of the "Fort Pillow Massacre") was too surreal to be ignored.

Confederates represent a part of our history. Judge past figures by today's values, and our Capitol's "Statuary Hall" would become "Empty Pedestal Hall." Instead, consider Budapest's Memento Park. Rather than destroy statuary from the Communist era, the city moved it into one park as a "monument" to democracy's triumph.

"Lost Cause" mythology claims that Confederates seceded over self-determination. Ironically, as local populations today reevaluate who to memorialize, that argument is ascendant. Urban demographics will continue to shift, along with popular will, meaning that in the future if the people so desire, Davis and Lee may march back into town.

GARY W. GALLAGHER
John L. Nau III Professor of History
Director, John L. Nau III Center for Civil War History

University of Virginia debates about the Civil War's memorial landscape erupt periodically and usually feature the same arguments from those who want to leave the statues and other monuments in place and those who want to remove them. How to deal with Confederate monuments inspires honest disagreement among well-intentioned, well-informed people, as well as some vitriolic cant from both ends of the political spectrum. In my view, eliminating parts of the memorial landscape is tantamount to destroying documents or images—all compose parts of the historical record and should be interpreted as such. I favor adding text that places monuments within the full sweep of how Americans have remembered the Civil War. I also support erecting new monuments devoted to previously slighted groups or events. The controversy over the equestrian statue of Robert E. Lee in Charlottesville is a good example of current debates. I would preserve the statue, add panels discussing its history, rename the park, and commission a memorial to the more than 250 men born in Albemarle County who served in United States Colored Troops units. Visitors to the revamped park could ponder generational changes in memorialization that underscore the contested nature of historical memory. Taking down statues, in contrast, potentially inhibits a real understanding of our past, wars and all, and can obscure important themes, movements, and eras.

LESLEY J. GORDON
Charles G. Summersell Chair of Southern History
University of Alabama

In 1908, the town of Raymond, in Hinds County, Mississippi, held
a ceremony to dedicate a monument to Confederate soldiers. Ex-
Confederate captain William T. Ratliff assured listeners that their
monument was not about defeat but instead courage and "principles
that would endure forever to show what men and women would do
for a cause they believed just and right." The Nathan Bedford Forrest
Chapter of the United Daughters of the Confederacy officially unveiled the statue, with an estimated 1,500 in attendance.

This statue, like the thousands found throughout the South and
beyond, had a clear message: to celebrate and promote the ideals
of the Lost Cause. The triumphant narrative of Confederate val-
or and sacrifice was meant to bolster white supremacy and silence
African American voices as much as their agency, particularly in
the context of the Jim Crow South.

This campaign of obfuscation has been remarkably successful,
leaving many white Americans unwilling or disinterested in grappling with the war's painful legacy. The removal of Confederate
monuments—and the vigorous debate it has inspired—helps, I believe, to finally reach some sort of reckoning with that past in order
to embrace a more pluralistic American society.

D. SCOTT HARTWIG
Supervisory Historian, retired
Gettysburg National Military Park

We are all aware that the legacy of our Civil War and Reconstruction
is complex, controversial, and for some, painful. I can understand
the anger residents of New Orleans might feel about a monument

in the heart of their city commemorating and celebrating an 1866 massacre of black citizens who were simply demonstrating for the right to vote. It was a constant reminder of a white supremacist society and I sympathize with the city's decision to remove it.

Monument removal, however, becomes more problematic when we apply it to any monument or memorial associated with the Confederacy, as if by removing these symbols we can somehow repair the past and heal wounds. But does it? It seems more likely to heal one wound and open another. A better solution to tearing down Confederate monuments is the example of the Arthur Ashe monument on Monument Avenue in Richmond. Ashe's monument reminds visitors and residents that Richmond's history is complicated and more than just the memory of the Confederacy and its leaders. Rather than tear down monuments, build new ones, where appropriate, that tell the story of those who struggled bravely for freedom and equality.

HAROLD HOLZER
Jonathan F. Fanton Director
Hunter College's Roosevelt House Public Policy Institute
Vice Chairman
The Lincoln Forum

A few years ago, my fellow historians Gary Gallagher and Joan Waugh took me to view the Indian War Monument in downtown Santa Fe. There, the problem of how to contextualize a tribute to the white man's battles against "savage Indians" was addressed by the almost comical obliteration of the adjective "savage."

The effort may have been clumsy, but it may point the way to contextualizing Confederate tributes, however ill conceived, without destroying artworks that may have both historical and aesthetic value. Some of the equestrian "icons" long on view in Richmond, for example, surely deserve to survive as stellar examples of American sculpture. Not all art is easy to digest.

But even Stalin did not order the destruction of the great statues of the tsars in St. Petersburg, though his own images suffered a far worse fate (and deserved no rescue, if only because they were so mediocre). In effect, I remain torn. I abhor the iconoclastic destruction of art—whether by the Taliban at Bamiyan, Afghanistan [where two monumental sculptures of Buddha were blown up in 2001], or by our own justifiably offended citizens in New Orleans. Using the preservation of a mediocre Jefferson Davis statue to rally neo-Nazis waving the Stars and Bars is a repugnant exercise that deserves condemnation. Do no local museums exist in these cities willing to reinstall, or properly label, the worthiest examples of the post–Civil War memorial movement?

ROBERT K. KRICK
Noted speaker on Civil War topics
Author of *Stonewall Jackson at Cedar Mountain*

We live in an age riven by shrill and intemperate voices, from all perspectives and on most topics. No sane person today would embrace, endorse, or tolerate slavery.

A casual observer, readily able to convince himself that he would have behaved similarly in the 1860s, can vault to high moral ground with the greatest of ease. Doing that gratifies the powerful self-righteous strain that runs through all of us, for better or worse. In fact, it leaps far ahead of the federal politicians (Lincoln among them) who said emphatically that slavery was not the issue, and millions of northern soldiers who fought, bled, and died in windrows to save the Union—but were noisily offended by mid-war emancipation.

It is impossible to imagine a United States in the current atmosphere that does not include zealots eager to obliterate any culture not precisely their own, destroying monuments in the fashion of Soviets after a purge, and antiquities in the manner of ISIS. The trend is redolent of the misery that inundated the planet during the aptly named Dark Ages, arising from savages who believed, as a matter of religion in that instance, that anyone with opinions different than their own was not just wrong, but craven and evil, and must be brutalized into conformity.

On the other hand, a generous proportion of the country now, and always, eschews extremism, and embraces tolerance of others' cultures and inheritances and beliefs. Such folk will be society's salvation.

MICHAEL J. MCAFEE
Curator of History
West Point Museum

In Saratoga National Military Park there is a monument bearing the sculpted image of a boot and an epaulette of a brigadier general. That general's name is not mentioned on the monument, nor is it on the series of plaques honoring generals of the American Revolution in the Old Cadet Chapel at West Point, New York. Despite his gallant service, that man turned his back on his cause and became a traitor. For that reason there are no monuments that mention the name Benedict Arnold.

What does this have to do with the southern monuments honoring the political and military leaders of the Confederacy? They, like Arnold, were traitors. They turned their backs on their nation, their oaths, and the sacrifices of their ancestors in the War for Independence. They did so not out of a sense of mistreatment or for money as did Arnold. They attempted to destroy their nation to defend chattel slavery and from a sense that as white men they were innately superior to all other races. They fought for white racial supremacy.

That is why monuments glorifying them and their cause should be removed. Leave monuments marking their participation on the battlefields of the war, but tear down those that only commemorate the intolerance, violence, and hate that inspired their attempt to destroy the American nation.

JOSEPH McGILL
Founder
The Slave Dwelling Project

This nation was founded on an underpinning of slavery and white supremacy. While President Thomas Jefferson penned in the Declaration of Independence that "all men are created equal," he owned six hundred people and fathered children with his enslaved Sally Hemings.

President James Madison is considered the father of our Constitution—"We the people." But Madison also owned slaves. The fact is, twelve of our former presidents owned slaves, and eight of them owned slaves while they were in office.

In our efforts to sanitize history by removing Confederate monuments that are reminders of slavery and white supremacy, we must ask ourselves: Where do we stop? As an African-American male, I do not buy into the "Heritage not Hate" defense of Confederate flags and monuments.

That said, I am in support of Confederate monuments remaining on the landscape. My reason being, Confederate soldiers were defending a way of life that was passed down to them. If we remove Confederate monuments, then we should also remove the monuments of their fathers and the fathers before them. In this sanitizing of history, we will eventually get to our Founding Fathers, some of whom were slave owners. How would Washington, D.C., look without the Washington Monument or the Jefferson Memorial?

MEGAN KATE NELSON
Independent Scholar
Author of *Ruin Nation: Destruction and the American Civil War*

What unites all of the participants in the debate about Confederate memorials? The belief that "retain" or "remove" are only two options. But what about a third option?

I would like to propose that Confederate memorials should neither be retained nor removed: They should be destroyed, and their broken pieces left in situ.

On a scheduled day, a city government or university administration would invite citizens to approach a Confederate memorial, take up a cudgel, and swing away. The ruination of the memorial would be a group effort, a way for an entire community to convert a symbol of racism and white supremacy into a symbol of resistance against oppression.

Historians could put up a plaque next to the fragments, explaining the memorial's history, from its dedication day to the moment of its obliteration. A series of photographs or a YouTube video could record the process of destruction. These textual explanations may be unnecessary, however. Ruins tend to convey their messages eloquently in and of themselves. In this case, the ruins of Confederate memorials in cities across the nation would suggest that while white supremacists have often made claims to power in American history, those who can oppose them can, and will, fight back.

ETHAN S. RAFUSE
Professor of History
U.S. Army Command and General Staff College
Fort Leavenworth, Kansas

Like Ulysses S. Grant, I respect the sacrifices and hardships the common soldier of the Confederacy endured, and the character and military skill of some of their leaders, while also disagreeing with those who wish to pay homage to the cause they fought for. Say what you will about the Civil War North (and much can be said that is critical), it did fight to preserve the ability of the United States to be a force for good in the world—and did so successfully. You also have to be pretty obtuse not to appreciate there is good reason to be offended by anything that honors people who fought to defend slavery and the southern racial order.

That being said, I cannot help but think the time and energy being devoted to the removal of monuments could be spent in more constructive ways. Moreover, like it or not, these monuments are part of our heritage and cultural landscape (warts and all) and have value as educational tools. I would not want to see the Confederate White House bulldozed or lose the fodder for discussion the Heyward Shepherd memorial at Harpers Ferry provides. Shepherd, the first man killed by John Brown's raiders, was African American. Thus, there is the very real, practical question in regards to the removal of monuments of where one stops—and who decides where that point is?

THOS. V. STRAIN JR.
Commander-in-Chief
Sons of Confederate Veterans

I was contacted by the editor of *Civil War Times* about my thoughts on the removal of monuments that have been erected to honor the men that fought for the Confederacy during the War Between the States. It is my opinion, and that of many others, that these removals are an attempt to erase history. If you take the time to read the comments on social media and on the websites of the news organizations reporting these removals it is obvious that only a few people actually support the removals. What it boils down to is that the politicians are telling those that elected them their wishes mean absolutely nothing to them.

Just this week one of these politicians that voted to remove a statue in Virginia lost in the primary for reelection and he noted that his stance on the removal more than likely cost him the election. In the end what we really have, in my humble opinion, is a group of people who are following their own personal agendas and saying, "to hell with the people" and moving forward with these removals. It isn't what we want, it is all about them.

SUSANNAH J. URAL
Professor of History
Codirector of the Dale Center for the Study of War and Society
University of Southern Mississippi

There's an obelisk at Karnak built to honor Hatshepsut, one of the few women pharaohs of ancient Egypt. Its inscription captures her curiosity at how she, who ushered in a period of prosperity and peace, would be remembered: "Now my heart turns this way and that, as I think what the people will say. Those who see my monuments in years to come, and who shall speak of what I have done." Hatshepsut's successor, for reasons still debated, nearly destroyed every memory of her. But history has a way of haunting us.

In an era of great division, most factions in the Confederate monuments debate actually agree that history should not be erased. The question is in how it should be remembered. In my opinion, if citizens come together and agree to remove the monuments, they should do so. But don't hide them away in warehouses. Place them at museums or battlefield parks where historians and interpreters can help visitors learn about the motives behind the Lost Cause. That movement erected these statues to, yes, honor concepts of sacrifice for liberty and family, but these monuments were also designed to entrench a ruthless tradition of white supremacy.

Like Hatshepsut's obelisk, Confederate memorials "speak of what [we] have done." Let us do just that at historic sites designed for that purpose, where Confederate symbols, including the flag, are and should be part of the landscape from which visitors learn.

The Largest Confederate Monument in America Can't Be Taken Down

It Has to Be Renamed, State by State

KEVIN WAITE

Washington Post, August 22, 2017

● The deep irony of a major highway in California and the Northwest honoring the only president of the Confederate States is highlighted in this analysis. Any alteration of the highway's name is a mighty challenge—one intended to perplex reformers, as historian Kevin Waite tries to untangle the issues in his opinion piece.

The largest monument to the Confederacy is not made of bronze. It's paved in asphalt.

For over a century, portions of America's road system have paid tribute to a failed slaveholding rebellion in the form of the Jefferson Davis Highway. Once planned as a single transcontinental highway, a series of roads that today bear Davis's name run for hundreds of miles through the South, while dozens of markers to the original highway are spread out across the country—from Virginia through the old Cotton Belt, then westward across Texas, New Mexico, Arizona, and into California.

Cutting through the southern half of the country, the Jefferson Davis Highway serves as a reminder that the fight over Civil War memory took place not only in the statues dotting parks across

America but in the very infrastructure of the nation itself. The highway is an asphalt monument to false equivalency, designed to balance the Lincoln Highway in the North with a Confederate rival in the South. It reveals the extent to which activists in the early twentieth century embedded their defense of the Confederacy in the growing infrastructure of the country.

The origins of this road system date to 1913, when the United Daughters of the Confederacy (UDC) unveiled their plans for a coast-to-coast highway in honor of the rebel chieftain. The project was intended as a rival of sorts to the then recently announced Lincoln Highway from New York to San Francisco, which was backed by northern capital. Not to be outdone by Yankee entrepreneurs, the UDC sketched out a southern analogue that would stretch from Arlington, Virginia, to San Diego—what writer Erin Blakemore recently called a "superhighway of Confederate veneration." The sectional animosities of the Civil War era thus lived on in the mapping of America's first national highway systems.

The time was ripe for such a massive monument to Davis. As the Daughters of the Confederacy went about promoting their highway, historical revisionists had sparked something of a white southern renaissance. In 1915, D. W. Griffith's *Birth of a Nation* hit theaters, reducing African Americans to crude caricatures while portraying the Ku Klux Klan as heroic defenders of white society. Despite NAACP protests, the film was a runaway success, even earning a screening in the White House. Later that year, the KKK reorganized at Stone Mountain, Georgia, and soon chapters began popping up across the country.

The South was rising again—in theaters, in vigilante organizations and, as the Daughters of the Confederacy hoped, through transcontinental infrastructure.

Yet the highway ultimately fell short of its architects' ambitions. Although the UDC claimed that their road ran the length of the country by the early 1920s, the maps of the period gave conflicting reports. Certainly no present-day U.S. road atlas will list the Jefferson Davis Highway as the continuous thoroughfare that the Daughters of the Confederacy had originally envisioned.

The reasons are complicated, but they stem from attempts to systematize America's road network in the mid-1920s. By that point, private organizations like the UDC had designated more than 250 named trails across the country. For motorists attempting to navigate the United States, this was a dizzying array of routes. In response, federal and state officials replaced the names of all interstate roads with a new numbering system. The Jefferson Davis Highway thus became U.S. 1, U.S. 15, U.S. 29, U.S. 80, and U.S. 90, among others. Similarly, the Lincoln Highway was superseded, primarily, by U.S. 80.

But because individual states still controlled the roads that passed through them, the UDC and other private organizations saw an opportunity. By lobbying state governments, the Daughters of the Confederacy could literally put Jefferson Davis back on the map. And these cash-strapped governments in need of new infrastructure, especially in the South, welcomed tributes to the old rebel president.

The fruits of those lobbying efforts, carried out over several decades, can be seen in dozens of Davis Highway markers across the country and in long stretches of road that still bear the Confederate president's name.

The Jefferson Davis Highway, for instance, runs through part of Virginia and then along the entire length of North Carolina and South Carolina. A number of markers line the roads of Georgia, while a long portion of the highway cuts through the heart of Alabama. Texas alone contains more than twenty markers to Davis's road.

West of the former Confederate states, the Jefferson Davis Highway continues. Parts of the I-10 through New Mexico still carry the name, as does a stretch of highway in Arizona. In California, Davis Highway markers can be found in several municipalities. The Daughters of the Confederacy extended the highway system as far north as Washington State, where Route 99 was named for Davis in the 1930s. In 2016, the state legislature and transportation commission finally renamed the road in honor of a black Civil War veteran.

Had he lived into the twentieth century, this is precisely the sort of infrastructural undertaking that Davis himself would have spearheaded. As a U.S. senator and secretary of war, Davis was one of the nation's most outspoken advocates for a transcontinental railroad during the antebellum period. He lobbied aggressively for a railway that would run through the Deep South and into California. Through railroad construction, Davis hoped to bind the slave South and the Far West and to extend the cotton economy to the Pacific coast. Abolitionists aptly dubbed this imagined railway "the great slavery road."

Davis, of course, never got his great slavery road. But in the extensive highway network that bears his name, Davis's nineteenth-century vision received a twentieth-century reboot of sorts. Taken together, the numerous segments of the Jefferson Davis Highway represent one of the signal accomplishments of Lost Cause revisionism, an enduring tribute to rebellion. This is a Confederate monument that spans the continent.

Yet the sprawling nature of the highway exposes pressure points for anti-Confederate activists to target. In Arlington, the highway's eastern terminus, county officials are seeking to remove Davis's name from their local thoroughfare. At the highway's original western terminus of San Diego, a plaque to Davis was removed just last week. Also last week, one of the highway markers in Arizona was tarred and feathered—clearly by someone with a flair for historical shaming rituals.

The most famous repurposing of the highway, however, occurred well before the recent white supremacist riot in Charlottesville. In March 1965, the Reverend Martin Luther King Jr. led protesters on a historic march along a fifty-four-mile stretch of the Jefferson Davis Highway between Selma, Alabama, and the state capital of Montgomery—where Davis himself had established the first White House of the Confederacy roughly a century earlier. When the march ended, tens of thousands of people gathered around the Capitol building to hear King's vision for a future free of racial injustice.

"The end we seek is a society at peace with itself, a society that can live with its conscience," King proclaimed in one of his most lyrical and hopeful speeches. "I know you are asking today: How long will it take? I come to say to you this afternoon however difficult the moment, however frustrating the hour, it will not be long. . . . Not long, because the arc of the moral universe is long, but it bends toward justice."

Yet vestiges of the old racial order that the Confederacy fought to preserve proved more resilient than even King himself could have expected. Three years later, he would be shot dead by a white assassin.

And the road that he and others marched along a half-century ago in their quest for civil rights? It's still the Jefferson Davis Highway.

Historian on "Confederate Kentucky"
Time to Remove the Statues

ANNE MARSHALL

Lexington Herald-Leader, August 16, 2017

● Historian Anne Marshall's methodical analysis of why and when Confederate statues need to be disappeared from the landscape, particularly in her home state of Kentucky, makes a powerful case for demolition.

Late Saturday, prompted by events in Virginia, Mayor Jim Gray announced he would expedite the removal of two Confederate monuments from the lawn of the former Fayette County courthouse.

The likenesses of John Hunt Morgan and John C. Breckenridge have been public targets since the deadly shooting in Charleston, South Carolina, in 2015 underscored the connection between Confederate symbolism and racial violence. But violence in Charlottesville added a new sense of immediacy.

As one who has studied the history of Confederate monuments in Kentucky, I was, as recently as a couple of years ago, advocating against this very thing. I was then committed to what historians and others call "contextualism." Contextualism aims, through historical explanation, to displace the original intent of the statues, which was to honor the Confederate Lost Cause.

As I argue at length in my book, *Creating a Confederate Kentucky*, whites erected Confederate monuments not only to remember the past but to control the present.

Initiated in an age where African Americans sought to make social, economic, and political gains, the monuments were a powerful reminder of who was in power. It was no coincidence that most appeared between 1890 and 1915, the heyday of lynching and the dawn of Jim Crow.

Historians and others who adopt this approach understand how and why Confederate monuments are offensive but argue that physically removing them from public places constitutes an erasure and a white washing of history. Instead, they advocate adding the voices of the oppressed to the historical landscape through signage, markers, and other statues representing the stories and experiences of slavery and Jim Crow.

My views changed, however, after seeing the failure of such a strategy in Louisville.

In 2012, the University of Louisville christened Freedom Park, a model example of contextualization. Designed by both historians and community members, the park includes multiple interpretive panels, which present and honor the struggle for black freedom over the course of the city's history. It was designed to counter the message of white power in the form of the hulking Confederate monument just across the street.

In my mind, it should have worked. Presenting the history of oppression and resilience of African Americans should have denuded the Confederate monument of its power as a symbol of the city's history and, accordingly, its meaning in the present.

But it did not. In a present in which racial injustice pervades the everyday life of so many, it turns out that no amount of historical context is particularly helpful. The public continued to protest and the city and the university responded by removing the statue last year.

Contextualization in public spaces doesn't work because monuments speak not only to who had power in the past, but who has it in the present. This is evident in the aggrieved voices who call for their removal. It is also clear from the voices of the white supremacists in Charlottesville who, in their cries of "You will not replace us," rallied not so much for Robert E. Lee, as much as against the broader attack on white power and identity this removal represents.

In times like these, removing Confederate monuments from public places is not an erasure of history but rather a statement by the cities and towns which choose to move them that the values for which the Confederacy stood before and after the war no longer represent them.

Some may see removing them as disrespectful of history or the people who lived it. But we should never honor or valorize people of history at the expense of the fellow humans we live amongst today. To prize the past over the present is to fetishize it and to create false idols of our ancestors.

Removing Confederate statues from places of public honor will not solve the injustices of today, but it is at least a powerful step in acknowledging them. We can hope that real acts of reform will follow the symbolic, and that bare earth and empty pedestals left by removed statues will not leave a void, but rather space for real change.

Anne E. Marshall, a Lexington native, is an associate professor at Mississippi State University.

The "Silent Sam" Confederate Monument at UNC Was Toppled. What Happens Next?

ETHAN J. KYTLE AND BLAIN ROBERTS

New York Times, August 21, 2018

● In the wake of several spontaneous removals of Confederate statues from their prominent places within public spaces, scholars contemplate the chain of events that has shaped the current crisis over what looms ahead. A spate of unauthorized topplings of monuments has created ongoing controversies over the "fate of the empty base," confronted by Ethan Kytle and Blain Roberts, professors of history at California State University, Fresno, in this reflective commentary.

On Monday evening, a small group of protesters used a rope to pull down "Silent Sam," the embattled Confederate statue that since 1913 had sat in a prominent spot on the campus of the University of North Carolina at Chapel Hill. They were part of a crowd of about 250 people who had marched through the center campus to the monument, unfurling banners, one of which read: "The whole world is watching. Which side are you on?"

But what should happen to the dislodged statue and the empty base?

As scholars of Civil War memory and UNC alumni, we hope that the monument will be placed in a museum, where it can be preserved and accurately interpreted as a white supremacist symbol. We also believe the statue's stone base should remain standing as a ruin—an empty pedestal laden with meaning.

UNC administrators long resisted calls to take down "Silent Sam," noting that state law tied their hands. But mounting criticism made their inaction untenable. Confederate monuments, after all, glorify men who fought to break apart the United States and create a nation dedicated to the maintenance of slavery. Yet Confederate monuments obscure this history, thereby perpetuating the Lost Cause lie that slavery was not the central cause of the Civil War. In short, they're bad history.

Most of these statues were erected during the Jim Crow era, when white southerners reasserted their racial dominance. The statues sanctioned the return of white supremacy and the violence at its core. Consider how a Confederate veteran bragged to the audience at the dedication of "Silent Sam" in 1913: "One hundred yards from where we stand," he said, "I horsewhipped a negro wench, until her skirts hung in shreds."

We once believed that Confederate statues should be left up but also placed in historical context. In 2015, we argued that they're artifacts that teach us important lessons about the segregated South, not the Civil War. We urged that Confederate monuments be supplemented with plaques that clarified their historical evasions, Jim Crow origins, and white supremacist function.

Over time, however, we lost our enthusiasm for this approach because it prioritizes pedagogical concerns over the experiences of African American residents.

The white supremacist intent of these monuments, in other words, is not a relic of the past. The Ku Klux Klan and neo-Nazi rally in Charlottesville, Virginia, last year underscored this point in blood. That horrifying demonstration in defense of the town's Robert E. Lee statue ended in the death of a counterprotester and the injury of many more. Now that these monuments have become totems for a resurgent white nationalist movement, the case for their removal is more urgent.

Still, removing a statue from the physical space that determined its significance and potency is its own kind of loss.

White southerners erected these monuments in city parks and on courthouse lawns and university campus quads. The prominence of the memorials shows how white southerners etched racism into the earth with impunity.

How do we preserve evidence of that? How do we preserve evidence that these monuments were inescapable? How do we show that generations of African Americans were forced to encounter them day after day? The perniciousness of location matters. This is why one of the best proposals for dealing with problematic monuments—removing them and placing them in museums, where they can be properly interpreted—is an imperfect solution.

Instead of complete removal, cities, towns, and colleges like UNC should consider taking down their Confederate statues but leaving the pedestals in place.

Historians such as Megan Kate Nelson and Kevin Levin have advocated this approach, or versions of it. Removing a monument but leaving behind an empty pedestal—shorn all original images and inscriptions—eliminates the offending tribute while still preserving a record of what these communities did and where they did it.

And the visual would stop people in their tracks. "What happened?" they might ask. "What used to be here? Why was it taken down?" Think of this proposal as a better version of contextualization. Text explaining the history of the monument and the decision to bring it down might still be added, but the pedestal would provide a more compelling commentary than even a new plaque.

That's what happened in New Orleans, which removed its Confederate statues in the spring of 2017. The sight of the soaring pedestal that once held up Robert E. Lee dominates the downtown skyline, demanding attention. Yet over the next few months, officials and residents will determine the fate of the empty base.

Another example of this at Duke University, which announced last week that it will not return its Lee statue to the space in the university chapel where it stood until 2017. As Duke's president observed, the void left behind makes "a powerful statement about the past, the present and our values."

The University of North Carolina should emulate its archrival and make the ruin a permanent part of the campus. The most effective way to commemorate the rise and fall of white supremacist monument-building is to preserve unoccupied pedestals as the ruins that they are—broken tributes to a morally bankrupt cause.

Bibliography

WEBSITES

The Southern Poverty Law Center maintains one of the most comprehensive and reliable sites for tracking Confederate statues and the status of these many hundreds of memorials. The site is part of a larger network of social justice initiatives featured on the SPLC *website.*

"Whose Heritage: Public Symbols of the Confederacy." https://www
.splcenter.org/20180604/whose-heritage-public-symbols-confederacy.

The Confederate Wave promotes Confederate heritage and connects to several other pro-Confederate resources, including nearly a dozen websites.

"Southern Heritage Confederate Information." http://www.confederatewave
.org/wave/southern-heritage.phtml.

VIDEOS

"Confederate Monuments." Organization of American Historians
Annual Meeting, Sacramento, Calif., 13 April 2018. C-SPAN. https://
www.c-span.org/video/?443541-1/confederate-monuments.

Confederate Monuments. Season 3, Episode 2, 18 August 2017. PBS.
https://www.pbs.org/video/confederate-monuments-qvlcxg/.

"Debate over Confederate Monuments." C-SPAN, 28 July 2018. https
://www.c-span.orgsearch/?searchtype=All&query=Confederate
+Monuments.

"James Grossman on Removal of Confederate Monuments." C-SPAN, 20
August 2017. https://www.c-span.org/video/?432763-4/washington
-journal-james-grossman-discusses-battle-confederate-monuments.

"Panel on Civil War Monuments and Memorials." American Civil War
Museum's 2017 annual symposium Lightning Rods of Controversy:
Civil War Monuments Past, Present, and Future, Richmond, Va., 25

February 2017. C-SPAN. https://www.c-span.org/video/?423748-105/panel-civil-war-monuments-memorials.

BOOKS

Allison, David B. *Controversial Monuments and Memorials: A Guide for Community Leaders*. New York: Rowan and Littlefield, 2018.

Brown, Thomas J. *Civil War Canon: Sites of Confederate Memory in South Carolina*. Chapel Hill: University of North Carolina Press, 2015.

———. *The Public Art of Civil War Commemoration: A Brief History with Documents*. Boston: Bedford / St. Martin's, 2004.

Driggs, Sarah Shields, Richard Guy Wilson, and Robert P. Winthrop. *Richmond's Monument Avenue*. Chapel Hill: University of North Carolina Press, 2001.

Fahs, Alice, and Joan Waugh, eds. *The Memory of the Civil War in American Culture*. Chapel Hill: University of North Carolina Press, 2004.

Friend, Craig Thompson, and Lorri Glover, eds. *Death and the American South*. New York: Cambridge University Press, 2015.

Gallagher, Gary. *Lee and His Army in Confederate History*. Chapel Hill: University of North Carolina Press, 2001.

Gallagher, Gary, and Alan T. Nolan. *The Myth of the Lost Cause and Civil War History*. Bloomington: Indiana University Press, 2000.

Hagler, Gould B. *Georgia's Confederate Monuments in Honor of a Fallen Nation*. Macon, Ga.: Mercer University Press, 2014.

Horton, James, and Lois Horton. *Slavery and Public History: The Tough Stuff of American Memory*. New York: New Press, 2006.

Jewell, K. Sue. *From Mammy to Miss America and Beyond: Cultural Images and the Shaping of U.S. Social Policy*. New York: Routledge, 1993.

Kreiser, Lawrence A. *The Civil War in Popular Culture: Memory and Meaning*. Lexington: University Press of Kentucky, 2006.

Landrieu, Mitch. *In the Shadow of Statues: A White Southerner Confronts History*. New York: Viking, 2018.

Levinson, Sanford. *Written in Stone: Public Monuments in Changing Societies*. Durham, N.C.: Duke University Press, 1998.

McElya, Micki. *Clinging to Mammy: The Faithful Slave in Twentieth-Century America*. Cambridge, Mass.: Harvard University Press, 2007.

Mills, Cynthia, and Pamela H. Simpson. *Monuments to the Lost Cause: Women, Art, and the Landscapes of Southern Memory*. Knoxville: University of Tennessee Press, 2003.

Roberts, Diane. *The Myth of Aunt Jemima: Representations of Race and Region*. New York: Routledge, 1994.

Savage, Kirk. *Standing Soldiers, Kneeling Slaves: Race, War, and Monument in Nineteenth-Century America*. Princeton, N.J.: Princeton University Press, 1997.

Sedore, Timothy Stephen. *An Illustrated Guide to Virginia's Confederate Monuments*. Carbondale: Southern Illinois University Press, 2011.

Towns, W. Stuart. *Enduring Legacy: Rhetoric and Ritual of the Lost Cause*. Tuscaloosa: University of Alabama Press, 2012.

Turner, Patricia. *Ceramic Uncles and Celluloid Mammies: Black Images and Their Influence on Culture*. New York: Anchor Books, 1994.

Wallace-Sanders, Kimberly. *Mammy: A Century of Race, Gender, and Southern Memory*. Ann Arbor: University of Michigan Press, 2008.

Whites, LeeAnn. *Gender Matters : Civil War, Reconstruction, and the Making of the new South*. New York: Palgrave, 2005.

ARTICLES

Baker, Bruce E. "Memory and the War: A Civil War Sesquicentennial Review." *Tennessee Historical Quarterly* 70 (Spring 2011): 52–59.

Bardes, John. "'Defend with True Hearts unto Death': Finding Historical Meaning in Confederate Memorial Hall." *Southern Cultures* 23 (Winter 2017): 29–45.

Bauman, Dan, and Clara Turnage. "We're Tracking Confederate Monuments: Tell Us What's on Your Campus." *Chronicle of Higher*

Education, 22 August 2017. https://www.chronicle.com/article
/We-re-Tracking-Confederate/240967.

Best, Wallace. "Mama and the Confederate Flag." *Callaloo* 24 (Winter
2001): 14–17.

Birkner, Michael J. "Monuments Ought to be Considered Case by Case."
LancasterOnline, 20 August 2017. https://lancasteronline.com
/opinion/columnists/monuments-ought-to-be-considered-case-by
-case/article_65667d02-8370-11e7-9bce-9f883bf7c5c7.html.

Bischof, Günter. "Why Not a Confederate Theme Park?" *New Orleans
Advocate*, 20 August 2015. http://www.theadvocate.com/baton
_rouge/opinion/our_views/article_a65869c2-cb87-5e74-acbb
-ddaf70a72925.html.

Bishir, Catherine W. "Landmarks of Power: Building a Southern Past,
1885–1915." *Southern Cultures* 1 (Spring 1993): 5–45.

———. "Memorial Observances." *Southern Cultures* 15, no. 2 (Summer
2009): 61–85.

Black, Bill. "Celebrating Nathan Bedford Forrest Is Celebrating White
Supremacy." *MLK50 Memphis*, 12 July 2017. https://mlk50.com
/celebrating-nathan-bedford-forrest-is-celebrating-white-supremacy
-25a8aa2cd815.

Blakemore, Erin. "The Lost Dream of a Superhighway to Honor the
Confederacy." *The Atlantic*, 29 August 2017. https://www.theatlantic
.com/business/archive/2017/08/jefferson-davis-highways/538062/.

Blight, David. "The Civil War Lies on Us like a Sleeping Dragon:
America's Deadly Divide—and Why It Has Returned." *The Guardian*,
20 August 2017. https://www.theguardian.com/us-news/2017
/aug/20/civil-war-american-history-trump.

Bonner, Robert E. "Flag Culture and the Consolidation of Confederate
Nationalism." *Journal of Southern History* 68 (May 2002): 293–332.

Boseman, Julie, "Battle over Confederate Monuments Moves to the
Cemeteries." *New York Times*, 21 September 2017. https://www
.nytimes.com/2017/09/21/us/confederate-monuments-cemeteries.
html.

Broun, Bill. "Why Confederate Monuments Should Be Removed from Gettysburg." *Morning Call*, 20 August 2017. http://www .mcall.com/opinion/yourview/mc-confederate-monuments -gettysburg-broun-yv-0818-20170819-story.html.

Brundage, W. Fitzhugh. "Contentious and Collected: Memory's Future in Southern History." *Journal of Southern History* 75 (August 2009): 751–66.

———. "I've Studied Confederate Memorials: Here's What to Do about Them." *Vox.com*, 18 August 2017. https://www.vox.com/the-big-idea /2017/8/18/16165160/ confederate-monuments-history-charlottesville-white-supremacy.

Burns, Michael. "A Confederate Memorial the 'Equal of Gettysburg': Sectionalism and Memory in the Establishment of Manassas National Battlefield Park, 1890–1940." *Virginia Magazine of History and Biography* 123, no. 2 (2015): 140–70.

Carbone, Christopher. "Which Confederate Statues Were Removed: A Running List." *Fox News*, 21 August 2017. http://www.foxnews.com /us/2018/03/11/which-confederate-statues-were-removed-running -list.html.

Carpenter, Lucas. "Old Times There Are Best Forgotten: The Future of Confederate Symbolism in the South." *Callaloo* 24 (Winter 2001): 32–37.

Casteel, Kathryn, and Anna Maria Barry-Jester. "There Are Still More than 700 Confederate Monuments in the U.S." *FiveThirtyEight*, 16 August 2017. https://fivethirtyeight.com/features/there-are-still-more -than-700-confederate-monuments-in-the-u-s/.

Chatelain, Marcia. "How Universities Embolden White Nationalists." *Chronicle of Higher Education*, 17 August 2017. https://www.chronicle .com/article/How-Universities-Embolden/240956.

Comegna, Anthony, "Debasing Roger Taney." *Libertarianism.org*, 21 August 2017. https://www.libertarianism.org/columns/debasing -roger-taney.

Cox, Karen. "The Confederacy's 'Living Monuments.'" *New York Times*, 6 October 2017. https://www.nytimes.com/2017/10/06/opinion /the-confederacys-living-monuments.html.

———. "The Whole Point of Confederate Monuments Is to Celebrate White Supremacy." *Washington Post*, 16 August 2017. https://www .washingtonpost.com/news/posteverything/wp/2017/08/16/the -whole-point-of-confederate-monuments-is-to-celebrate-white -supremacy/?utm_term=.fbdb1ed4865e.

———. "Why Confederate Memorials Must Fall." *New York Times*, 15 August 2017. https://www.nytimes.com/2017/08/15/opinion /confederate-monuments-white-supremacy-charlottesville .html?_r=0.

Dailey, Jane. "The Confederate General Who Was Erased." *Huffington Post*, 21 August 2017. https://www.huffingtonpost.com/entry /the-confederate-general-who-was-erased-from-history_us _599b3747e4b06a788a2af43e.

De Groot, Jerome. "Monuments to the Past." *History Today*, 17 August 2017. https://www.historytoday.com/jerome-de-groot /monuments-past.

Dubenko, Anna. "Right and Left on Removal of Confederate Statues." *New York Times*, 18 August 2017. https://www.nytimes.com /2017/08/18/us/politics/right-and-left-on-removal-of -confederate-statues.html.

Edwards, Laura. "Why Confederate Statues Fail to Represent Southern History." *The Hill*, 23 August 2017. http://thehill.com/blogs /pundits-blog/civil-rights/347630-why-confederate-statues-fail -to-represent-southern-history.

Foner, Eric. "Confederate Statues and 'Our' History." *New York Times*, 20 August 2017. https://www.nytimes.com/2017/08/20/opinion /confederate-statues-american-history.html.

Forts, Franklin. "Living with Confederate Symbols." *Southern Cultures* 8 (Spring 2002): 60–75. https://muse.jhu.edu/article/30950.

Goodheart, Adam. "Regime Change in Charlottesville." *Politico*, 16 August 2017. https://www.politico.com/magazine/story/2017/08/16 /regime-change-in-charlottesville-215500.

Gordon-Reed, Annette. "Charlottesville: Why Jefferson Matters." *New York Review of Books*, 19 August 2017. https://www.nybooks .com/daily/2017/08/19/charlottesville-why-jefferson -matters/.

Graham, David A. "The Stubborn Persistence of Confederate Monuments." *The Atlantic*, 26 April 2016. https://www.theatlantic .com/politics/archive/2016/04/the-stubborn-persistence-of -confederate-monuments/479751/.

Greenberg, Amy, Karen Cox, James Grossman, Peniel Joseph, Kevin Levin, Jane Censer, Richard Poplak, and Sisonke Msimang. "Historians: 'Defending History Is Complicated in the U.S.'" *CNN Opinion*, 19 August 2017. https://www.cnn.com/2017/08/19/opinions /historians-confederate-statues-opinion-roundup/index.html.

Gunter, Booth, Jamie Kizzire, and Cindy Kent, "Whose Heritage? Public Symbols of the Confederacy." *SPLC Special Report*, Southern Poverty Law Center, 21 April 2016. https://www.splcenter.org /20180604/whose-heritage-public-symbols-confederacy.

Hague, Euan, and Edward H. Sebesta. "The Jefferson Davis Highway: Contesting the Confederacy in the Pacific Northwest." *Journal of American Studies* 45 (May 2011): 281–301.

Handley-Cousins, Sarah. "Falling out of Love with the Civil War." *Nursing Clio*, 21 August 2017. https://nursingclio.org/2017/08/21 /falling-out-of-love-with-the-civil-war/.

Hillyer, Reiko. "Relics of Reconciliation: The Confederate Museum and Civil War Memory in the New South." *Public Historian* 33 (November 2011): 35–62.

Holpuch, Amanda, and Mona Chalabi. "'Changing History'? No-32 Confederate Monuments Dedicated in Past 17 Years." *The Guardian*, 16 August 2017. https://www.theguardian.com/us-news/2017/aug/16 /confederate-monuments-civil-war-history-trump.

Hosmer, Brian. "Trauma, Reconciliation, and Historical Responsibility." *Reconciliation Annual Symposium*, May 2016. https://brianhosmer

.wordpress.com/2017/08/18/trauma-reconciliation-and-historical
-responsibility/.

Hwang, Kyung Moon "Monuments Are Not Untouchable." *Korea
Times*, 30 August 2017. http://www.koreatimes.co.kr/www/opinion
/2017/08/638_235681.html.

Janney, Caroline E. "War over a Shrine of Peace: The Appomattox Peace
Monument and Retreat from Reconciliation." *Journal of Southern
History* 77, no. 1 (February 2011): 91–120.

Kurtz, Hilda E. "Introduction to the Special Forum: In the Aftermath of
the Hate Rally in Charlottesville." *Southeastern Geographer* 58, no. 1
(Spring 2018): 6–8.

Lande, Jonathan. "'Confederate Monuments . . . What to Do?':
Historians' Town-Hall Meeting on Memorialization—and Racial
Injustice." *Muster*, 27 April 2018. https://journalofthecivilwarera
.org/2018/04/confederate-monuments-historians-town-hall-meeting
-memorialization-racial-injustice/.

Lanktree, Graham. "Racism in America: Should the U.S. Get Rid of All
Confederate Monuments?" *Newsweek*, 9 September 2017. https
://www.newsweek.com/should-america-rid-itself-confederate
-monuments-661991.

Leib, Jonathan I., Gerald R. Webster, and Roberta H. Webster. "Rebel
with a Cause? Iconography and Public Memory in the Southern
United States." *GeoJournal* 52 (January 2000): 303–10.

Levin, Kevin M. "Confederate Monuments Syllabus." *Civil War Memory*.
http://cwmemory.com/civilwarmemorysyllabus/.

———. "Why I Changed My Mind about Confederate Monuments."
The Atlantic, 19 August 2017. https://www.theatlantic.com/politics
/archive/2017/08/why-i-changed-my-mind-about-confederate
-monuments/537396/.

Levin, Kevin M., and Fred L. Borch. "Has the Lost Cause Lost?" *Wilson
Quarterly* 34 (Summer 2010): 7–10.

Levitz, Jennifer. "Daughters of Confederacy 'Reeling' from Memorial
Removals." *Wall Street Journal*, 21 August 2017. https://www.wsj.com

/articles/daughters-of-confederacy-reeling-from-memorial-removals
-1503307806.

Lewis, Sarah. "Which Is the Real Confederate Flag?" *New York Times*, 25
June 2017. https://www.nytimes.com/2017/06/25/us/confederate
-flag-civil-war.html?mtrref=www.google.
com&gwh=E0A04D1C883E2AAF08D7B00B2FF97574&gwt=pay.

Little, Becky. "How the U.S. Got So Many Confederate Monuments."
History Stories, 17 August 2017. https://www.history.com/news
/how-the-u-s-got-so-many-confederate-monuments.

Marshall, Anne E. "Historian on 'Confederate Kentucky': Time to
Remove the Statues." *Lexington-Herald*, 16 August 2017. https://www
.kentucky.com/opinion/op-ed/article167643757.html.

Marten, Jim. "Thoughts on Confederate Monuments." *Historians@
Work*, 23 August 2017. https://marquettehistorians.wordpress.com
/2017/08/23/thoughts-on-confederate-monuments-my-own
-and-others/.

Meacham, Jon. "Why Lee Should Go, and Washington Should Stay."
New York Times, 21 August 2017. https://www.nytimes.com/2017
/08/21/opinion/why-lee-should-go-and-washington-should-stay
.html?_r=0.

Merritt, Keri Leigh. "Charlottesville and the Confederate Legacy."
Moyers and Company, 17 August 2017. http://billmoyers.com/story
/charlottesville-confederate-legacy/.

Mitchell, Mary Niall. "A Tale of Two Cities: New Orleans and the Fight
over Confederate Monuments." *History*, 11 May 2017. https://www
.history.com/news/a-tale-of-two-cities-new-orleans-and-the-fight
-over-confederate-monuments.

Nelson, Megan Kate. "Transforming White Supremacist Memorials: Two
Proposals." *Historista*, 15 August 2017. http://www.megankatenelson
.com/transforming-white-supremacist-memorials-two-proposals/.

Newson, Ryan Andrew. "Epistemological Crises Made Stone:
Confederate Monuments and the End of Memory." *Journal of the
Society of Christian Ethics* 37, no. 2 (Fall/Winter 2017): 135–51.

Oberg, Michael Leroy. "On Charlottesville, and Our National
    Character." *Native America: A History*, 13 August 2017.
    http://michaelleroyoberg.com/red-lives-matter/on-charlottesville
    -and-our-national-character/.

Panhorst, Michael W. "Devotion, Deception, and the Ladies Memorial
    Association, 1865–1898: The Mystery of the Alabama Confederate
    Monument." *Alabama Review* 65, no. 3 (2012): 163–204.

Raymond, Adam K. "A Running List of Confederate Monuments
    Removed across the Country." *New York Magazine*, 25 August 2017.
    http://nymag.com/daily/intelligencer/2017/08/running-list-of
    -confederate-monuments-that-have-been-removed.html.

Roberts, Blain, and Ethan J. Kytle. "Looking the Thing in the Face:
    Slavery, Race, and the Commemorative Landscape in Charleston,
    South Carolina, 1865–2010." *Journal of Southern History* 78, no. 3
    (2012): 639–84.

———. "Unsure about Confederate Statues: Ask Yourself If You
    Support White Supremacy." *Fresno Bee*, 16 August 2017. https://www
    .fresnobee.com/opinion/readers-opinion/article167609442.html.

Rubin, Louis D. "Of Statuary, Symbolism, and Sam." *Callaloo* 24, no. 1
    (2001): 160–61.

Ruck, Joanna. "Confederate Statues Removed across Southern U.S.
    States." *The Guardian*, 15 August 2017. https://www.theguardian.com
    /us-news/gallery/2017/aug/15/confederate-statues-removed
    -across-southern-us-states-in-pictures.

Safo, Nick. "Are Confederate Monuments Important Works of Art?"
    ArtDaily.org. http://artdaily.com/news/98198/Are-Confederate
    -monuments-important-works-of-art—#.Wrxwh44wti2.

Schmidt, Jalane. "Excuse Me, America Your House Is on Fire: Lessons
    from Charlottesville on the KKK and 'alt-right.'" *Medium*, 27 June
    2017. https://medium.com/resist-here/excuse-me-america-your-house
    -is-on-fire-lessons-from-charlottesville-on-the-kkk-and-alt-right
    -84aafddca685.

Schuessler, Jennifer. "Historians Question Trump's Comments on Confederate Monuments." *New York Times*, 15 August 2017. https://www.nytimes.com/2017/08/15/arts/design/trump-robert -e-lee-george-washington-thomas-jefferson.html.

Shorter, David. "The Fragile Statues of Whiteness." *Huffington Post*, 28 August 2017. https://www.huffingtonpost.com/entry/the-fragile -statues-of-whiteness_us_59981418e4b033e0fbdec456.

Silber, Nina. "Worshiping the Confederacy Is about White Supremacy—Even the Nazis Thought So." *Washington Post*, 17 August 2017. https://www.washingtonpost.com/news/made-by -history/wp/2017/08/17/worshiping-the-confederacy-is-about-white -supremacy-even-the-nazis-thought-so/?utm_term=.dbc52733da73.

Sinha, Manisha. "What Those Monuments Stand For." *New York Daily News*, 18 August 2017. http://www.nydailynews.com/opinion /monuments-stand-article-1.3423887.

Upton, Dell. "Confederate Monuments and Civic Values in the Wake of Charlottesville." *Society of Architectural Historians*, 13 September 2017. https://www.sah.org/publications-and-research/sah-blog/sah-blog /2017/09/13/confederate-monuments-and-civic-values-in-the-wake -of-charlottesville.

Ural, Susannah J. "Let Us Speak of What We Have Done." *Reflections on War and Society*, 28 July 2017. https://dalecentersouthernmiss .wordpress.com/2017/07/28/let-us-speak-of-what-we-have-done/.

Waite, Kevin. "The Largest Confederate Monument in America Can't Be Taken Down." *Washington Post*, 22 August 2017. https://www .washingtonpost.com/news/made-by-history/wp/2017/08/22 /the-largest-confederate-monument-in-america-cant-be-taken-down /?utm_term=.390381717433.

———. "A Museum of Confederate Statues Could Help End the American Civil War." *The Conversation*, 24 August 2017. http://theconversation.com/a-museum-of-confederate-statues -could-help-end-the-american-civil-war-82934.

Walker, Katherine D. "United, Regardless, and a Bit Regretful: Confederate History Month, the Slavery Apology, and the Failure of Commemoration." *American Nineteenth Century History* 9, no. 3 (September 2008): 315–38.

Ward, Jason. "The Myth of Southern Blood." *Washington Posts*, 21 August 2017. https://www.washingtonpost.com/news/made-by-history/wp/2017/08/21/the-myth-of-southern-blood/?utm_term=.5f188765a089.

Whites, LeeAnn. "Confederate Rock and Roll: Civil War Commemoration and Lived History." *Journal of the Midwest Modern Language Association* 45 (Spring 2012): 11–15.

Williams, Chad. "Donald Trump: The Neo-Confederate President." *Cassius*, 17 August 2017. https://cassiuslife.com/18975/donald-trump-the-neo-confederate-president/.

Winberry, John J. "'Lest We Forget': The Confederate Monument and the Southern Townscape." *Southeastern Geographer* 55, no. 1 (Spring 2015): 19–31.

Zimmerman, Jonathan. "The Civil War, Race, and the Whitewashing of History." *Newsday*, 14 August 2017. https://www.newsday.com/opinion/commentary/the-civil-war-race-and-the-whitewashing-of-history-1.14030467.

———. "The Progressive Case for Keeping Confederate Statues Standing: We Shouldn't Cart Away Reminders to Our White Supremacist History." *New York Daily News*, 21 August 2017. http://www.nydailynews.com/opinion/progressive-case-keeping-confederate-statues-standing-article-1.3429164.

Alabama

Fox, Justin. "What Confederate Monument Builders Were Thinking: Southern Leaders Made It Clear That Statues Were Part of Their Early 20th-Century Effort 'to Establish White Supremacy.'" *Bloomberg*, 20 August 2017. https://www.bloomberg.com/view/articles/2017-08-20/what-confederate-monument-builders-were-thinking.

Gattis, Paul. "Alabama's Confederate Monuments: 'Good, Bad and Ugly' of Heritage or Hate Fight." *Birmingham Real-Time News*, 19 August 2017. http://www.al.com/news/birmingham/index.ssf/2017/08/alabama_gov_kay_ivey_says_the.html.

Graham, David A. "Local Officials Want to Remove Confederate Monuments—but States Won't Let Them." *The Atlantic*, 25 August 2017. https://www.theatlantic.com/politics/archive/2017/08/when-local-officials-want-to-tear-down-confederate-monuments-but-cant/537351/.

Johnson, Alex. "A New Confederate Monument Goes Up in Alabama." *NBC News*, 27 August 2017. https://www.nbcnews.com/news/us-news/new-confederate-monument-goes-alabama-n796531.

Kazek, Kelly. "A Look at Confederate Monuments in Every Alabama County." *Alabama Living*, 17 August 2017, updated 8 January 2018. http://www.al.com/living/index.ssf/2017/08/here_are_confederate_monuments.html.

Luckerson, Victor. "Dismantling Dixie: The Summer the Confederate Monuments Came Crashing Down." *The Ringer*, 17 August 1017. https://www.theringer.com/2017/8/17/16160286/charlottesville-richmond-montgomery-confederate-monuments.

Okeowo, Alexis. "Witnessing a Rally for a New Confederate Monument." *New Yorker*, 29 August 2017. https://www.newyorker.com/culture/culture-desk/witnessing-a-rally-for-a-brand-new-confederate-monument.

Arizona

Farzan, Antonia Noori. "Someone Turned the Confederate Memorial at
the Capitol into a Second-Place Trophy." *Phoenix New Times*, 16
August 2017. http://www.phoenixnewtimes.com/news/activist-turns
-confederate-memorial-at-arizona-capitol-into-participation-trophy
-9596953.
Gundran, Robert, and Gabriella Del Rio. "Arizona Confederate
Monument Tarred and Feathered." *USA Today*, 18 August 2017.
https://www.usatoday.com/story/news/nation-now/2017/08/18
/arizona-confederate-monument-tarred-feathered/579232001/.

Arkansas

Christ, Mark K. "Arkansas Listings in the National Register of Historic
Places: Fayetteville National Cemetery and Fayetteville Confederate
Cemetery." *Arkansas Historical Quarterly* 71 (Summer 2012): 217–21.
Latimer, Franklin Allen. "Arkansas Listings in the National Historical
Places: The Confederate Soldiers Monument and Monument to
Confederate Women in Little Rock." *Arkansas Historical Association*
60 (Autumn 2001): 305–10.

California

Waite, Kevin. "The Struggle over Slavery Was Not Confined to the
South, L.A. Has a Confederate Memorial Problem Too." *Los Angeles
Times*, 4 August 2017. http://www.latimes.com/opinion/op-ed/la-oe
-waite-socal-confederates-20170804-story.html.

Colorado

Washington, Danika. "A History of Racism, The KKK, and Crimes
against American Indians: Colorado's Struggle with Divisive
Monuments Started Long Ago." *Denver Post*, 18 August 2017.
https://www.denverpost.com/2017/08/18/confederate-monuments
-statues-kkk-racism-charlottesville-colorado/.

Florida

"Florida to Replace Confederate Statue in U.S. Capitol with Civil-Rights
    Leader Mary McLeod Bethune." *Orlando Sentinel*, 19 March 2018.
    http://www.orlandosentinel.com/news/breaking-news/os-scott
    -signs-bills-bethune-statue-20180319-story.html.
Gabriel, Melissa Nelson. "Supporters of Pensacola's Confederate
    Monument Plan Rally in Lee Square." *Pensacola News Journal*,
    21 August 2017. https://www.pnj.com/story/news/2017/08/21
    /pensacola-confederate-monument-rally-lee-square/586261001/.
Miami Herald Editorial Board. "Educator Mary McLeod Bethune
    Deserves to Represent Florida." *Miami Herald*, 21 March 2018. http
    ://www.miamiherald.com/opinion/editorials/article206152264.html.
Phillips, Shayla. "Florida Civil-Rights Leader Mary McLeod Bethune
    Will Replace Confederate Statue in the U.S. Capitol." *Orlando Weekly*,
    21 March 2018. https://www.orlandoweekly.com/Blogs
    /archives/2018/03/21/florida-civil-rights-leader-mary-mcleod
    -bethune-will-replace-confederate-statue-in-the-us-capitol.

Georgia

Boissoneault, Lorraine. "What Will Happen to Stone Mountain,
    America's Largest Confederate Memorial?" *Smithsonian*, 22 August
    2017. https://www.smithsonianmag.com/history/what-will-happen
    -stone-mountain-americas-largest-confederate-memorial-180964588/.
Edwards, Johnny. "NAACP Will Protest GA City's 'White and Fair'
    Confederate Monument." *Atlanta Journal-Constitution*, 22 August
    2017. https://www.myajc.com/blog/investigations/naacp-will
    -protest-city-white-and-fair-confederate-monument
    /EMX8QtGl3mcyHxPVvoSn2I/.
Grossman, James. "Whose Memory? Whose Monuments? History,
    Commemoration, and the Struggle for an Ethical Past." *Perspectives on
    History*, American Historical Association, February 2016. https
    ://www.historians.org/publications-and-directories/perspectives-on

-history/february-2016/whose-memory-whose-monuments-history
-commemoration-and-the-struggle-for-an-ethical-past.

Hale, Grace Elizabeth. "Granite Stopped Time: The Stone Mountain
Memorial and the Representation of White Southern Identity."
Georgia Historical Quarterly 82 (Spring 1998): 22–44.

Hendrix, Steve. "Stone Mountain: The Ugly Past—and Fraught
Future—of the Biggest Confederate Monument." *Washington Post*, 19
September 2017. https://www.washingtonpost.com/news/retropolis
/wp/2017/09/19/stone-mountain-the-ugly-past-and-fraught-future
-of-the-biggest-confederate-monument/?utm_term=.f46251917e44.

Martinez, J. Michael. "The Georgia Confederate Flag Dispute." *Georgia
Historical Quarterly* 92 (Summer 2008): 200–228.

Sinclair, Harriet. "Stone Mountain Confederate Memorial in Georgia
Has to Go, Democrat Gubernatorial Candidate Says." *Newsweek*, 16
August 2017. http://www.newsweek.com/confederate-mountain
-carving-must-go-georgia-gubernatorial-candidate-says-651679.

Wheeler, Frank. "'Our Confederate Dead': The Story behind Savannah's
Confederate Monument." *Georgia Historical Quarterly* 82 (Summer
1998): 382–97.

Zakos, Katharine P. "Truth Is Marching On: The Lasershow Spectacular
at the Stone Mountain Park Confederate Memorial and the Changing
Narratives of History." *Journal of Heritage Tourism* 10 (Spring 2015):
280–95.

Idaho

Newcomer, Daniel. "Lower Boise Historical Marker-Confederates in
Idaho." *Clio*, 31 January 2016. https://www.theclio.com/web
/entry?id=21447.

Illinois

Davenport, Cory. "A Walk down Rozier Street: Why Alton's
Confederate Monument Is Different." *RiverBender*, 31 August 2017.

https://www.riverbender.com/articles/details/a-walk-down-rozier
-street-why-altons-confederate-monument-is-different-23120.cfm.

Emmanuel, Adeshina. "How the South Side Came to House a Not-So-
Controversial Confederate Memorial." *Chicago Magazine*, 21
September 2017.

Moreno, Nereida. "Confederate Monument Stands on Chicago's South
Side as Questions Swirl around the Country." *Chicago Tribune*, 17
August 2017.

Parker, Molly. "Civil War 'Still with Us': Confederate Flag Still Prevalent
in Southern Illinois." *The Southern*, 11 July 2015. http://thesouthern
.com/news/local/confederate-flag-still-prevalent-in-southern-illinois
/article_311544a9-e25c-5cd5-8d33-7c668dec6891.html.

Slowik, Ted. "Chicago House Confederate Monument at Well-Known
Cemetery." *Chicago Tribune*, 15 August 2017. http://www
.chicagotribune.com/suburbs/daily-southtown/opinion/ct-sta
-slowik-confederate-mound-st-0816-20170815-story.html.

Iowa

Munson, Kyle. "'Stupid Liberals' vs. White Privilege: Iowa Caught Up in
Confederate Monuments Debate." *Des Moines Register*, 25 August
2017, updated 28 August 2017. https://www.desmoinesregister.com
/story/news/local/columnists/kyle-munson/2017/08/25/americas
-civil-war-over-confederate-monuments-takes-root-iowa/588650001/.

Murphy, Erin. "Locals Defend Iowa's Confederate Monuments as
National Debate Rages." *Quad-City Times*, 1 September 2017. http://
qctimes.com/news/state-and-regional/iowa/locals-defend-iowa-s
-confederate-monuments-as-national-debate-rages/article
_264570a6-58f5-5a11-897c-f843d8ef8a42.html.

Kentucky

Bailey, Phillip M. "Messy Mystery: Confederate Time Capsule Found."
Louisville Courier Journal, 21 November 2016. https://www

.courier-journal.com/story/news/local/2016/11/21/confederate
-monument-time-capsule-found/94229042/.

Louisiana

Hill, Jennifer. "The History and Enduring Legacy of Bloody Caddo."
   Bayou Brief, 13 December 2017. https://www.bayoubrief.com/2017/12
   /13/the-history-and-enduring-legacy-of-bloody-caddo/.
Loewen, James W. "The Monument to White Power That Still Stands
   in New Orleans." *History News Network*, 3 September 2015. https
   ://historynewsnetwork.org/blog/153667.
McDonald, Brent. "Taking a Knee and Taking Down a Monument."
   New York Times, 3 February 2018. https://www.nytimes.com/2018
   /02/03/us/taking-down-a-confederate-monument.html.
Rao, Sameer. "Kneeling Protests and Confederate Monuments Converge
   for Shreveport Family." *Colorlines*, 10 January 2018. https://www
   .colorlines.com/articles/watch-kneeling-protests-and-confederate
   -monuments-converge-shreveport-family.
Wendland, Tegan. "With Lee Statue's Removal, Another Battle of New
   Orleans Comes to a Close." National Public Radio, with WWNO
   Radio, 20 May 2017. https://www.npr.org/2017/05/20/529232823
   /with-lee-statues-removal-another-battle-of-new-orleans-comes-to
   -a-close.

Maine

Gallagher, Noel K. "Bowdoin Relocates Confederate Plaque." *Portland
   Press Herald*, 19 August 2017. https://www.pressherald.com/2017
   /08/19/bowdoin-college-is-moving-confederate-memorial-plaque/.
McDermott, Deborah. "Historian Debunks Theory of Confederate
   Statue in Maine." *Bangor Daily News*, 30 August 2017. http://
   bangordailynews.com/2017/08/30/news/york/historian-debunks
   -theory-of-confederate-statue-in-maine/.
Whittle, Patrick. "Maine Governor Says Removing Confederate Statues
   Is like Losing 9-11 Memorial." *Bloomberg*, 17 August 2017.

https://www.bloomberg.com/news/articles/2017-08-17/gov
-removing-confederate-statues-like-losing-9-11-memorial.

Maryland

Dailey, Jane. "Baltimore's Confederate Monument Was Never about
'History and Culture.'" *Huffington Post*, 17 August 2017. https
://www.huffingtonpost.com/entry/confederate-monuments
-history-trump-baltimore_us_5995a3a6e4b0d0d2cc84c952.

Mississippi

"Another Confederate Statue Sparks Debate in Mississippi." *U.S. News
& World Report*, 6 September 2017. https://www.usnews.com/news
/best-states/mississippi/articles/2017-09-06/another-confederate
-statue-sparks-debate-in-mississippi.

"Confederate Monuments: Mississippi Lawmaker's Resignation
Demanded." *Times Picayune*, 23 May 2017. http://www.nola.com
/politics/index.ssf/2017/05/mississippi_lawmaker_lynching.html.

Davis, Jack E. "A Struggle for Public History: Black and White Claims
to Natchez's Past." *Public Historian* 22 (Winter 2000): 45–63.

Neff, John, Jarod Roll, and Anne Twitty. "A Brief Historical
Contextualization of the Confederate Monument at the University of
Mississippi." University of Mississippi. https://history.olemiss.edu
/wp-content/uploads/sites/6/2017/08/A-Brief-Historical
-Contextualization-of-the-Confederate-Monument-at-the
-University-of-Mississippi.pdf.

Wall, Ezra. "NAACP Leader Calls for Removal of Confederate
Monuments." Mississippi Public Broadcasting, 11 August 2017.
http://www.mpbonline.org/blogs/news/2017/08/11/naacp-leader
-calls-for-removal-of-confederate-monuments/.

Missouri

Kansas City Star Editorial Board, "It's Time to Remove Kansas City's
Confederate Monument." *Kansas City Star*, 18 August 2017. http://

www.kansascity.com/opinion/editorials/article167868797
.html.

"Kansas City Takes Down Confederate Monument after Vandalism."
Reuters, 25 August 2017. https://www.reuters.com/article/us-usa
-protests-statues/kansas-city-takes-down-confederate-monument
-after-vandalism-idUSKCN1B51X2.

O'Neil, Tim. "Everything You Need to Know about the Confederate
Monument in Forest Park." *St. Louis Post-Dispatch*, 30 May 2017.
http://www.stltoday.com/news/local/govt-and-politics/everything-
you-need-to-know-about-the-confederate-monument-in/article
_bf090beb-965c-5f8b-bef1-e84fcc8646a6.html.

Serhan, Yasmeen. "St. Louis to Remove Its Confederate Monument."
The Atlantic, 26 June 2017. https://www.theatlantic.com/news
/archive/2017/06/st-louis-to-remove-its-confederate-monument
/531720/.

Montana

Knauber, Al. "Helena Works to Explain Its Confederate Memorial as
Other Cities Take Theirs Down." *Helena Independent Record*, 21 May
2017. http://helenair.com/news/local/helena-works-to-explain-its
-confederate-memorial-as-other-cities/article_2507b1bd-e354
-5f30-a56d-84130fe620eb.html.

Michels, Holly K. "American Indian Group Calls for Removal of
Helena's Confederate Monument." *Helena Independent Record*, 15
August 2017. http://helenair.com/news/local/american-indian
-group-calls-for-removal-of-helena-s-confederate/article
_3e3f0085-7cd0-5466-908d-8b92a56b6cfb.html.

New York

Reverby, Susan. "This Doctor Experimented on Slaves: It's Time to
Remove or Redo His Statue." *Hastings Center*, 7 August 2017.

Short, Aaron. "From the Bronx to Brooklyn, Confederate Symbols
Come Down across New York City." *Hyperallergic*, 22 August 2017.

https://hyperallergic.com/397022/confederate-symbols-removed
-nyc/.

Smith, Greg B. "A Look at NYC's Contentious Statues as Uproar over
Removal Mounts." *New York Daily News*, 2 September 2017.
http://www.nydailynews.com/new-york/city-remove-nyc-iconic
-statues-article-1.3464427.

Sullivan Robert. "It's Hard to Get Rid of a Confederate Memorial in
New York City." *New Yorker*, 23 August 2017. https://www.newyorker
.com/culture/culture-desk/its-hard-to-get-rid-of-a-confederate
-memorial-in-new-york-city.

North Carolina

Eanes, Zachary. "Durham Confederate Statue: Tribute to Dying
Veterans or Political Tool of Jim Crow South?" *News and Observer*, 16
August 2017. http://www.newsobserver.com/news/local/counties
/durham-county/article167672037.html.

Graham, David A. "Durham's Confederate Statue Comes Down." *The
Atlantic*, 15 August 2017. https://www.theatlantic.com/politics
/archive/2017/08/durhams-civil-war-monument-and
-the-backlash-to-the-backlash/536889/.

Jenkins, Nash. "A Confederate Statue Is Gone, but the Fight Remains in
Durham." *Time*, 16 August 2017. http://time.com/4902514/durham
-confederate-statue-future/.

Katz, Jonathan M. "Protestor Arrested in Toppling of Confederate
Statue in Durham." *New York Times*, 15 August 2017. https://www
.nytimes.com/2017/08/15/us/protester-arrested-in-toppling-of
-confederate-statue-in-durham.html.

"Monument Timemap." Temporal and Spatial Mapping of North
Carolina Commemorative Landscapes. DocSouth. http://docsouth
.unc.edu/commland/explore/timemap/.

Sexton, Scott. "Winston-Salem's Confederate Monument Should No
Longer Be Ignored." *Winston-Salem Journal*, 15 August 2017.
http://www.journalnow.com/news/columnists/scott_sexton/sexton

-winston-salem-s-confederate-monument-should-no-longer-be
/article_7e097132-45f1-53be-b203-ca44f2b42838.html.

Vincent, Tom. "Evidence of Woman's Loyalty, Perseverance, and
Fidelity: Confederate Soldiers' Monuments in North Carolina, 1865–
1914." *North Carolina Historical Review* 83, no. 1 (2006): 61–90.

Warren-Hicks, Colin, and Jane Stancill. "UNC Chapel Hill Puts Fence
around Silent Sam Confederate Statue Before Tuesday Rally." *Herald
Sun*, 22 August 2017. http://www.heraldsun.com/news/local
/counties/orange-county/article168578842.html.

Ohio

Raymond, Adam K. "A Confederate Monument Taken Down in Ohio
Will Return after Public Outcry." *New York Magazine*, 28 September
2017. http://nymag.com/daily/intelligencer/2017/09/a-confederate
-monument-taken-down-in-ohio-will-return.html.

Oklahoma

"Confederate Monument Removed from Oklahoma Elementary
School." *Washington Post*, 21 March 2018.

Felder, Ben. "Oklahoma Has at Least 2 Dozen Confederate
Monuments." *Tulsa World*, 20 August 2017. http://www.tulsaworld
.com/homepagelatest/oklahoma-has-at-least-dozen-confederate
-monuments/article_f15c452e-7125-5920-a6c9-79f3831f5e1a
.html.

Pennsylvania

Levy, Dustin B. "Gettysburg Park Officials: Confederate Monuments
Here to Stay." *Hanover Evening Sun*, 15 August 2017. https://www
.eveningsun.com/story/news/2017/08/15/gettysburg-park-official
-confederate-monuments-here-stay/567986001/.

Rhode Island

Naylor, Donita. "Confederate States Stand on Revered Westerly
Granite." *Providence Journal*, 22 September 2017. http://www

.providencejournal.com/news/20170922/confederate-statues
-stand-on-revered-westerly-granite.

South Carolina

"#Charlestonsyllabus." African American Intellectual History Society.
https://www.aaihs.org/resources/charlestonsyllabus/.
Waters, Darin. "Whose Story? Democratizing America's Collective
Historical Memory." *Mountain Xpress*, 16 June 2014. https://
mountainx.com/opinion/whose-story-democratizing-americas
-collective-historical-memory/.

Tennessee

Connolly, Daniel, and Vivian Wang. "Confederate Statues in Memphis
Are Removed after City Council Vote." *New York Times*, 20 December
2017. https://www.nytimes.com/2017/12/20/us/statue-memphis
-removed.html.
Jaschik, Scott. "Lost Cause No Longer." *Inside Higher Education*, 16
August 2016. https://www.insidehighered.com/news/2016/08
/16/vanderbilt-pays-back-donation-daughters-confederacy
-so-it-can-remove-confederate.
Sit, Ryan. "Confederate Monument of a KKK Leader Was Only Just
Removed in Memphis." *Newsweek*, 21 December 2017. http://www
.newsweek.com/confederate-monuments-removal-memphis
-tennessee-jim-crow-civil-right-755233.
Sutton, Benjamin. "Memphis Takes Down Two Confederate
Monuments, Including Statue of KKK Leader." *Hyperallergic*, 21
December 2017. https://hyperallergic.com/418499/memphis-takes
-down-two-confederate-monuments/.

Texas

Blanchard, Bobby. "Texas Has More than 180 Public Symbols of the
Confederacy: Explore Them Here." *Texas Tribune*, 21 August 2017.
https://www.texastribune.org/2017/08/21/texas-has-second-most
-public-symbols-confederacy-nation/.

Bova, Gus. "Who's Defending Texas' Confederate Monuments?"
    Texas Observer, 30 October 2017. https://www.texasobserver.org
    /whos-defending-texas-confederate-monuments/.

Jarvie, Jenny. "As Monuments to the Confederacy Are Removed from
    Public Squares, New Ones Are Quietly Being Erected." *Los Angeles
    Times*, 22 October 2017. http://www.latimes.com/nation
    /la-na-new-confederate-memorials-20171020-story.html.

Jukam, Kelsey, John Savage, and Alisa Semiens. "The Hidden
    Confederate History of the Texas Capitol: Unofficial Guide." *Texas
    Observer*, 17 February 2015. https://www.texasobserver.org
    /hidden-confederate-history-texas-capitol-unofficial-guide/.

Kirk, Bryan. "Historic or Horrific: 178 Confederate Monuments Are
    Found in Texas." *Houston Patch*, 17 August 2017. https://patch.com
    /texas/houston/
    historic-or-horrific-178-confederate-monuments-are-found-texas.

Lomax, John Nova. "Coming Soon: A Large Confederate Memorial on
    I-10, Just Inside the Texas State Line." *Texas Monthly*, 7 April 2015.
    https://www.texasmonthly.com/the-daily-post/coming-soon-a
    -large-confederate-memorial-on-i-10-just-inside-the-texas-state-line/.

Savage, John. "Confederate Monument Protests Draw Hundreds in
    Houston and Dallas." *Texas Observer*, 19 August 2017. https://www
    .texasobserver.org/confederate-monument-protest-draws-hundreds
    -houston/.

Wolcott, Victoria W. "Six Flags Has Taken Down Its Confederate Flag.
    but That's Not the Only Legacy of Jim Crow at the Park." *Washington
    Post*, 28 August 2017. https://www.washingtonpost.com/news/made
    -by-history/wp/2017/08/28/six-flags-has-taken-down-its-confederate
    -flag-but-thats-not-the-only-legacy-of-jim-crow-at-the-park/?utm
    _term=.2a6508d587b5.

Austin

Bromwich, Jonah Engel. "University of Texas at Austin Removes
    Confederate Statues in Overnight Operation." *New York Times*, 21

August 2017. https://www.nytimes.com/2017/08/21/us/texas-austin
-confederate-statues.html.

Courtney, David. "Jefferson Davis Is Back at UT." *Texas Monthly*, 17
April 2017. https://www.texasmonthly.com/the-daily-post/jefferson
-davis-back-ut/.

Silver, Jonathan. "Why Texas Leaders Erected Confederate Monuments
at the Capitol." *Austin American-Statesman*, 13 October 2017. https
://www.statesman.com/news/why-texas-leaders-erected-confederate-
monuments-the-capitol/OYU6kxC8zIT5epA1mh8CRO/.

Dallas

Kennedy, Bud. "Why Robert E. Lee Memorial in Dallas May Be
Coming to Fort Worth Area." *Fort Worth Star-Telegram*,
20 March 2018. http://www.star-telegram.com/opinion
/opn-columns-blogs/bud-kennedy/article206104929.html.
(—The original title was "Dallas Confederate Memorial Might Land
in White Settlement." White Settlement is the name of a town near
Fort Worth.)

Phillips, Michael. "Dallas' Monuments to the Confederacy Must Come
Down." *Dallas Morning News*, 20 July 2017. https://www.dallasnews
.com/opinion/opinion/2017/07/20/dallas-monuments-confederacy
-must-come.

Schutze, Jim. "Confederate Statue Debate Has Been Great for Dallas,
Believe It or Not." *Dallas Observer*, 22 September 2017. http://www
.dallasobserver.com/news/the-confederate-statue-debate-is
-the-best-thing-that-ever-happened-to-dallas-9900965.

El Paso

Villa, Pablo. "Confederate Gen. Robert E. Lee's Name May Be Removed
from El Paso Landmarks." *El Paso Times*, 16 August 2017. https://
www.elpasotimes.com/story/news/politics/local/2017/08/16
/steps-start-remove-robert-e-lees-name-el-paso-landmarks
/573467001/.

Houston

Berman, Mark. "Texas Man Charged with Trying to Bomb a
   Confederate Statue in Houston." *Washington Post*, 21 August 2017.
   https://www.washingtonpost.com/news/post-nation/wp/2017/08/21
   /texas-man-charged-with-trying-to-bomb-a-confederate-statue-in
   -houston/?utm_term=.f4769f1f3f0f.

Martin, Florian. "So What about All Those Confederate Symbols in
   Houston?" *Houston Public Media*, 29 June 2015. https://www
   .houstonpublicmedia.org/articles/news/2015/06/29/61233
   /so-what-about-all-those-confederate-symbols-in-houston/.

McMurray, Cort. "Houston We Need To Talk about Those Confederate
   Statues." *Houston Chronicle*, 19 August 2017. https://www
   .houstonchronicle.com/local/gray-matters/article/How-Houston
   -s-Confederate-memorials-can-help-us-11943884.php.

San Antonio

Allen, Paula. "Who Paid to Have the Confederate Statue Made and
   Then Placed in the Park?" *San Antonio Express News*, 14 August 2017.
   https://www.expressnews.com/militarycity/article/Who-paid-to
   -have-the-Confederate-statue-in-Travis-11817622.php.

Contreras, Guillermo. "Group Sues San Antonio over Removal of
   Confederate Statue." *San Antonio Express News*, 25 October 2017.
   https://www.mysanantonio.com/news/local/article/Group-sues
   -San-Antonio-over-removal-of-12306414.php.

Dimmick, Iris. "Confederate Statue Defenders Lose Court Appeal
   in San Antonio." *Rivard Report*, 31 August 2017. https://
   therivardreport.com/confederate-monument-downtown-san-antonio
   -will-removed/.

Utah

"Utah College Returns Statue of Confederate Soldiers to Artist." *The
   Guardian*, 19 January 2015. https://www.theguardian.com
   /us-news/2015/jan/19/utah-college-returns-statue-confederate
   -soldiers-the-rebels-artist.

Virginia

Chornesky, Michael B. "Confederate Island upon the Union's 'Most Hallowed Ground': The Battle to Interpret Arlington House, 1921–1937." *Washington History* 27 (Winter 2015): 20–33.

Krowl, Michelle A. "'In the Spirit of Fraternity': The United States Government and the Burial of Confederate Dead at Arlington National Cemetery, 1864–1914." *Virginia Magazine of History and Biography* 111 (2003): 151–86.

Charlottesville

Duggan, Paul. Charlottesville Judge Orders Shrouds Removed from Confederate Statues." *Washington Post*, 27 February 2018. https://www.washingtonpost.com/local/crime/charlottesville-judge-orders-shrouds-removed-from-confederate-statues/2018/02/27/3592ae10-1bf6-11e8-9de1-147dd2df3829_story.html?utm_term=.8a9c87b1c1c9.

Gordon-Reed, Annette. "Charlottesville: Why Jefferson Matters." *New York Review of Books*, 19 August 2017. http://www.nybooks.com/daily/2017/08/19/charlottesville-why-jefferson-matters/.

Held, Amy. "Shrouds Pulled from Charlottesville Confederate Statues, Following Ruling." National Public Radio, 28 February 28 2018. https://www.npr.org/sections/thetwo-way/2018/02/28/589451855/shrouds-pulled-from-charlottesville-confederate-statues-following-ruling.

"History in Dispute: Charlottesville and Confederate Monuments." The Choices Program, Brown University. http://www.choices.edu/teaching-news-lesson/history-dispute-charlottesville-confederate-monuments/.

Kennedy, Maev. "Heather Heyer, Victim of Charlottesville Car Attack, Was a Civil Rights Activist." *The Guardian*, 13 August 2017. https://www.theguardian.com/us-news/2017/aug/13/woman-killed-at-white-supremacist-rally-in-charlottesville-named.

"Klan Members Rally against Removal of General Lee Statue in Virginia." *Reuters*, 8 July 2017. https://www.reuters.com/article

/us-virginia-klan/klan-members-rally-against-removal-of-general
-lee-statue-in-virginia-idUSKBN19T142.

Merritt, Keri Leigh. "Charlottesville and the Confederate Legacy."
Bill Moyers, 17 August 2017. http://billmoyers.com/story
/charlottesville-confederate-legacy/.

Nelson, Sophia A. "OpEd: Charlottesville Changed My Mind on
Removing Confederate Monuments." *NBC News Digital*, 13
September 2017. https://www.nbcnews.com/news/nbcblk/oped
-charlottesville-changed-my-mind-removing-confederate-monuments
-n796331.

Oppenheim, Maya. "KKK Grand Dragon Says I'm 'Glad' Heather Heyer
Died in Charlottesville." *The Independent*, 16 August 2017. https://
www.independent.co.uk/news/world/americas/kkk-leader
-charloteesville-im-glad-girl-dies-heather-heyer-killed-james-alex-fields
-jr-grand-dragon-a7895851.html.

Park, Madison. "Why White Nationalists Are Drawn to Charlottesville."
CNN, 12 August 2017. https://www.cnn.com/2017/08/11/us
/charlottesville-white-nationalists-rally-why/index.html.

Rankin, Claudia. "Was Charlottesville the Exception or the Rule?" *New
York Times*, 20 August 2017. https://www.nytimes.com/2017/09/13
/magazine/was-charlottesville-the-exception-or-the-rule
.html?mtrref=www.google.om&gwh=1C8B375B7E3CC9F0E47
EA0404D84D65D&gwt=pay.

Spencer, Hawes, and Sheryl Gay Stolberg. "White Nationalists March on
University of Virginia." *New York Times*, 11 August 2017. https://
www.nytimes.com/2017/08/11/us/white-nationalists-rally
-charlottesville-virginia.html.

Zeitz, Joshua. "What Happened in Charlottesville Is All Too American."
Politico, 13 August 2017. https://www.politico.com/magazine
/story/2017/08/13/what-happened-in-charlottesville-is-all-too
-american-215482.

Washington

Banel, Feliks. "Wrestling with the Ghosts of Confederate Monuments."
    MyNorthwest, 19 May 2017. http://mynorthwest.com/634176
    /wrestling-with-the-ghosts-of-confederate-monuments/.

DeMay, Daniel. "Wash. Confederate Monument along I-5: 'Racist
    Symbolism.'" *Seattle Pi*, 16 August 2017. https://www.seattlepi.com
    /seattlenews/article/Wash-Confederate-monument-along-I-5-Racist
    -11821079.php.

Fletcher, Phillis, Molly Solomon, and Courtney Flatt. "Northwest
    Confederate Monuments Targeted for Removal and Vandalism." *NW
    News Network*, 19 August 2017. http://nwnewsnetwork.org/post
    /northwest-confederate-monuments-targeted-removal-and
    -vandalism.

Kostanich, Kara. "Group Wants Confederate Monument Removed from
    Local Cemetery." *KOMO News*, 12 July 2015. http://komonews.com
    /archive/group-wants-confederate-monument-removed-from
    -local-cemetery.

McNamara, Neal. "A Confederate Flag Flies in Washington, and Its
    Caretaker Explains Why." *Seattle Patch*, 16 August 2017. https://patch
    .com/washington/seattle/confederate-flag-flies-washington
    -its-caretaker-explains-why.

Washington, D.C.

Lefrak, Mikaela. "Here Are the Confederate Monuments in Washington
    and Where They Stand." American University Radio, 18 August 2017,
    updated 25 September 2017. https://wamu.org/story/17/08/18
    /local-confederate-statues-stand/.

Subberwal, Kaeli. "D.C. Grapples with Its Own Confederate Statue
    Controversy after Charlottesville." *Huffington Post*, 15 August 2017.
    https://www.huffingtonpost.com/entry/confederate-statue
    -washington-dc-protests_us_59934d38e4b04b193360f21f.

Wisconsin

Lese, Chris. "Wisconsin Embraced Confederate History throughout the 20th Century." *Historicalese*, 15 October 2017. https://justdohistory .wordpress.com/2017/10/15/wisconsin-embraced-confederate -history-throughout-the-20th-century/.

Permissions Credits

"The Mammy Washington Almost Had," by Tony Horwitz, from *The Atlantic*, 31 May 2013, https://www.theatlantic.com/national /archive/2013/05/the-mammy-washington-almost-had/276431/, is reprinted by permission of Tony Horwitz and *The Atlantic*.

"More Than a Statue: Rethinking J. Marion Sims's Legacy," by Deidre Cooper Owens, from *Rewire*, 24 August 2017, https://rewire.news /article/2017/08/24/statue-rethinking-j-marion-sims-legacy/, is published with permission from Rewire.News.

"Confederate Monuments and Tributes in the United States, Explained," from *Teen Vogue*, 6 September 2017, https://www.teenvogue.com /story/confederate-monuments-and-tributes-in-the-united-states -explained, is reprinted by permission of the author.

"'The Civil War Lies on Us like a Sleeping Dragon': America's Deadly Divide—and Why It Has Returned," by David Blight, from *The Guardian*, 20 August 2017, https://www.theguardian.com/us-news /2017/aug/20/civil-war-american-history-trump, is reprinted by permission of Guardian News & Media Limited.

"Lincoln, Monuments, and Memory," by Harold Holzer, from *Civil War Times*, 21 November 2017, http://www.historynet.com/lincoln -monuments-memory-harold-holzers-remembrance-day-address.htm, is reprinted by permission of *Civil War Times Magazine*.

"Confederate Memorials: Their Past and Futures," by Jane Turner Censer, is reprinted by permission of the author.

"Empty Pedestals: What Should Be Done with Civic Monuments to the Confederacy and Its Leaders? by *Civil War Times*, appeared in the October 2017 issue, http://www.historynet.com/empty-pedestals

-civic-monuments-confederacy-leaders.htm, and is reprinted by
permission of *Civil War Times Magazine*.

"The Largest Confederate Monument in America Can't Be Taken
Down: It Has to Be Renamed, State by State," by Kevin Waite, from
the *Washington Post*, 22 August 2017, https://www.washingtonpost
.com/news/made-by-history/wp/2017/08/22/the-largest-confederate
-monument-in-america-cant-be-taken-down/?utm_
term=.54143d2eee7c, is reprinted by permission of the author.

"Historian on 'Confederate Kentucky': Time to Remove the Statues," by
Anne Marshall, from the *Lexington Herald-Leader*, 16 August 2017,
http://www.kentucky.com/opinion/op-ed/article167643757.html, is
reprinted permission of the *Lexington Herald-Leader* and the author.

"The 'Silent Sam' Confederate Monument at UNC Was Toppled. What
Happens Next?," by Ethan J. Kytle and Blain Roberts, from the *New
York Times*, 21 August 2018, https://www.nytimes.com/2018/08/21
/opinion/silent-sam-confederate-monument-north-carolina.html, is
reprinted by permission of the authors.